THE MUSICIAN'S GUIDE
TO AURAL SKILLS

THE MUSICIAN'S GUIDE TO AURAL SKILLS

Sight-Singing

FOURTH EDITION

Paul Murphy
Muhlenberg College

Joel Phillips
Westminster Choir College of Rider University

Elizabeth West Marvin
Eastman School of Music

Jane Piper Clendinning
Florida State University College of Music

W. W. NORTON & COMPANY
Independent Publishers Since 1923

W. W. Norton & Company has been independent since its founding in 1923, when William Warder Norton and Mary D. Herter Norton first published lectures delivered at the People's Institute, the adult education division of New York City's Cooper Union. The firm soon expanded its program beyond the Institute, publishing books by celebrated academics from America and abroad. By midcentury, the two major pillars of Norton's publishing program—trade books and college texts—were firmly established. In the 1950s, the Norton family transferred control of the company to its employees, and today—with a staff of five hundred and hundreds of trade, college, and professional titles published each year—W. W. Norton & Company stands as the largest and oldest publishing house owned wholly by its employees.

Fourth Edition

Editor: Christopher Freitag
Assistant editor: Julie Kocsis
Development editor: Meg Wilhoite
Project editor: Michael Fauver
Managing editor, College: Marian Johnson
Managing editor, College Digital Media: Kim Yi
Copyeditor: Jodi Beder
Proofreader: Debra Nichols
Media editor: Steve Hoge
Media assistant editor: Eleanor Shirocky
Production manager: Stephen Sajdak
Design director: Rubina Yeh
Designer: Marisa Nakasone
Music typesetting and page composition: David Botwinik
Manufacturing: Sheridan Books, Inc.

ISBN: 978-0-393-69709-4

W. W. Norton & Company, Inc., 500 Fifth Avenue, New York, NY 10110
www.wwnorton.com

W. W. Norton & Company, Ltd., 15 Carlisle Street, London W1D 3BS

1 2 3 4 5 6 7 8 9 0

Contents

Part III   Chromatic Harmony and Form

Part IV   The Twentieth Century and Beyond

A B A C A B A coda

Seven Part Rondo / Ternary

A B A C A   Five Part Rondo

A B A C A
        ↓
    Development

A   A   Strophic → Same music, different words

A B A C A coletta   5-Part Rondo

Preface

The Musician's Guide series is the most comprehensive set of materials available for learning music theory and aural skills. Comprising a theory text, Workbook, and Anthology, and two aural-skills texts, the series features coordinated resources that can be mixed and matched for any theory curriculum.

The Musician's Guide to Aural Skills consists of two volumes—*Sight-Singing* and *Ear-Training*. *Sight-Singing* emphasizes the skills required for real-time performance. It includes strategic, progressive training in melodic- and rhythm-reading, improvisation, composition, and keyboard skills. *Ear-Training* develops listening skills using two activities. Short ***Try it*** dictations focus on pattern recognition, and **Contextual Listening** exercises guide students in discovering those patterns when taking dictation from music literature. Both texts feature a wide range of real musical repertoire of diverse origins, including classical, popular, and folk selections. Though the ordering and terminology of these two texts correspond to *The Musician's Guide to Theory and Analysis*, they may be used together, individually, or in conjunction with other theory texts.

The Musician's Guide to Aural Skills: Sight-Singing is distinctive in three significant ways. First, since the inception of the Musician's Guide series, a primary goal has been to present literature from composers whose works are historically underrepresented. The fourth edition's literature significantly expands that gender, ethnic, racial, and geographical diversity with the addition of dozens of works, many of which have never before appeared in any pedagogical forum.

Second, this text emphasizes skills integration. These include the ability to imagine and perform the sounds of printed music; to recall music by singing, playing, and writing it; and to improvise and create new music in a variety of styles. For example, as preparation for singing rhythms and melodies in simple meter, Chapter 2 instructs students how to conduct simple duple meter as part of an exercise in which they point to notated rhythmic patterns while singing. They then improvise their own phrases using these same patterns in combinations of their own choosing. Finally, they notate their improvisations and exchange them with others to perform and evaluate.

Third, this text emphasizes collaboration. In addition to collaborative improvisations, there are many ensemble works—not only duets, but also music for three, four, and five parts. These range from the abundant two-part rhythms to be performed by a soloist or in pairs, to group singing, such as Daisy Allen's rag "A Bit O' Sunshine" in Chapter 28.

Using This Volume

Sight-Singing divides into 40 chapters that align with both *Ear-Training* and *The Musician's Guide to Theory and Analysis*. Thus, instructors will find it easy to plan for class and to coordinate aural skills with the concepts presented in written theory.

Each chapter begins with specific learning objectives and integrates melodic and rhythmic performances along with improvisation and keyboard exercises. Études help students acclimate to singing and conducting, recognize patterns, and interpret the elements of music notation. Moreover, they develop a sense of scale degree and intonation by applying solfège syllables or scale-degree numbers. Ideally, students will employ these études throughout their study as warm-ups, for syllable proficiency, and for vocal development. The vast majority of melodies, however, derive from a wide range of styles and periods—from popular (Broadway musicals, movies and television, classic rock, video games, jazz, and blues) to Common Practice, as well as twentieth- and twenty-first-century music literature.

Sight-Singing also features hundreds of carefully sequenced rhythm exercises. We begin with the basics of beat and meter. Later, we incorporate divided, subdivided, and doubled beats, mapping these concepts onto different beat values. We provide explanations and études for understanding dotted and tied notes, managing interruptions of the tempo, coordinating super-subdivided beats in slow tempos, performing different types of syncopation, understanding swung rhythms, internalizing characteristic jazz and ragtime rhythms through actual literature, and singing rhythms of the spoken word.

We conclude by presenting a great variety of techniques developed or revisited by composers of the twentieth and twenty-first centuries: ametric rhythms, serialized rhythms, feathered beams, added values, isorhythm, and non-retrogradable rhythms. With diagrams throughout, students receive guidance on conducting simple beat patterns while they perform rhythms.

The improvisation and keyboard activities found in every chapter, reinforcing key chapter concepts, are carefully scaffolded so that students who have little to no experience can succeed in developing these skills while having fun making music. These exercises may be performed as solos, with a partner, or in groups. We use the keyboard as a fundamental musical tool and a kinesthetic mnemonic, rather than for the purpose of developing pianists. The keyboard exercises spiral, often expanding earlier models to develop more-advanced concepts. For example, simple two-voice contrapuntal patterns recur as the soprano and bass of four-part exercises, and later with chromatic alterations.

Following most improvisations are *Quick Composition* exercises in which students notate their favorite improvisations to share with peers or the class for purposes of content mastery and analysis.

Planning Your Curriculum

The Musician's Guide covers concepts typically taught during the first two years of college instruction in music. We hope that instructors who adopt both the *Theory and Analysis* and *Aural Skills* texts will appreciate the consistent pedagogical approach, terminology, and order of presentation. Because students' aural and practical skills sometimes develop more slowly than their grasp of theoretical concepts, there is no harm done if aural and practical instruction trails slightly behind conceptual understanding. For this reason, we summarize the organization of the volumes and suggest strategies for using them. Deployed over four or five semesters, these two models coordinate with typical music theory college curricula.

Plan 1 (four semesters, including one semester dealing with musical rudiments)

	Sight-Singing	Ear-Training
Term 1	Chapters 1–10	Chapters 1–10
Term 2	Chapters 11–21	Chapters 11–21
Term 3	Chapters 22–33	Chapters 22–33
Term 4	Chapters 34–40	Chapters 34–40

Alternatively, the following organization is one suggestion for those curricula that offer a dedicated rudiments class in addition to a four-semester core sequence.

Plan 2 (a rudiments class followed by four semesters)

	Sight-Singing	Ear-Training
Rudiments	Chapters 1–8	Chapters 1–8
Term 1	Chapters 9–14	Chapters 9–14 (with review of modes from Chapter 5)
Term 2	Chapters 15–21	Chapters 15–21
Term 3	Chapters 22–33	Chapters 22–33
Term 4	Chapters 34–40	Chapters 34–40

Applying Solfège Syllables and Scale-Degree Numbers

All singing systems have merit and choosing *some* system is far superior to using none. To reinforce musical patterns, we recommend singing with movable-*do* solfège syllables and/or scale-degree numbers, but we provide a summary explanation of both the movable- and fixed-*do* systems in Chapter 1 to help students get started. (A quick reference for diatonic and chromatic syllables also appears at the front of this volume.) For solfège in modal contexts, we present two systems in Chapter 9, one using syllables derived from major and minor, and one using relative (rotated) syllables.

Applying a Rhythm-Counting System

Many people use some counting system to learn and perform rhythms—in effect, "rhythmic solfège." For example, a rhythm in $\frac{2}{4}$ meter might be vocalized "du de, du ta de ta" (Edwin Gordon system), or "1 and, 2 e and a" (McHose/Tibbs system), or "Ta di Ta ka di mi" (Takadimi system). We leave it to the discretion of each instructor whether to use such a system and which to require.

Our Thanks to . . .

A work of this size and scope is helped along the way by many people. We are especially grateful for the support of our families and our students. Our work together as coauthors has been incredibly rewarding, a collaboration for which we are sincerely thankful.

For subvention of the recordings, we thank James Undercofler (director and dean of the Eastman School of Music), as well as Eastman's Professional Development Committee. For audio engineering, we are grateful to recording engineers John Ebert and John Baker. For audio production work, we thank Glenn West, Christina Lenti, and Lance Peeler, who assisted in the recording sessions. We also thank our colleagues at both Westminster Choir College and the Eastman School of Music who gave of their talents to help make the recordings. The joy of their music making contributed mightily to this project.

We are grateful for the thorough and detailed work of our pre-publication reviewers, whose suggestions inspired many improvements, large and small: Erin Perdue Brownfield (East Ascension High School), Tracy Carr (Eastern New Mexico University), David Davies (Texas A&M University-Commerce), Amy Engelsdorfer (Luther College), Stefanie Harger Gardner (Glendale Community College, AZ), William Heinrichs (University of Wisconsin–Milwaukee), Ronald Hemmel (Westminster Choir College), Jennifer Jessen-Foose (Cedar Grove High School), Kimberly Goddard Loeffert (Oklahoma State University), Ryan Messling (Prairie High School), David Parker (Bob Jones University), Brian Parrish (Parkway West High School), Richard Robbins (University of Minnesota Duluth), Jennifer Russell (Northern Arizona University), Janna Saslaw (Loyola University), and Heather Thayer (Henderson State University). For previous editions, reviewers have included Michael Berry (University of Washington), David Castro

(St. Olaf College), Melissa Cox (Emory University), Gary Don (University of Wisconsin-Eau Claire), Jeff Donovick (St. Petersburg College), Terry Eder (Plano Senior High School), Jeffrey Gillespie (Butler University), Bruce Hammel (Virginia Commonwealth University), Melissa Hoag (Oakland University), Rebecca Jemian (University of Louisville), Charles Leinberger (University of Texas-El Paso), David Lockart (North Hunterdon High School), Robert Mills (Liberty University), Daniel Musselman (Union University), Kristen Nelson (Stephen F. Austin State University), Shaugn O'Donnell (City College, CUNY), Tim Pack (University of Oregon), Scott Perkins (DePauw University), Ruth Rendleman (Montclair State University), Sarah Sarver (Oklahoma City University), Alexander Tutunov (Southern Oregon University), and Annie Yih (University of California at Santa Barbara).

We are indebted to the staff of W. W. Norton for their commitment to this project and their painstaking care in producing these volumes. Most notable among these are Chris Freitag, who has capably guided this edition with great enthusiasm; Meg Wilhoite, who served as Development Editor; Justin Hoffman, who steered the second and third editions with a steady hand; and Maribeth Anderson Payne, whose vision helped launch the series with great aplomb. Michael Fauver was project editor of the volume, with assistance from copyeditor Jodi Beder and proofreader Debra Nichols. We appreciate the invaluable assistance of media experts Steve Hoge and Eleanor Shirocky. Julie Kocsis was assistant editor, David Botwinik was typesetter, and Stephen Sajdak was production manager.

Joel Phillips, Paul Murphy, Elizabeth West Marvin,
and Jane Piper Clendinning

THE MUSICIAN'S GUIDE
TO AURAL SKILLS

PART

I

Elements of Music

CHAPTER 1

Pitch and Pitch Class

In this chapter you'll learn to:

- Apply solfège syllables, scale-degree numbers, and letter names
- Improvise and compose melodies
- Evaluate sung performances of peer compositions
- Sing pitch-only melodies that feature both steps and skips
- Read melodies written in treble, bass, alto, and tenor clefs
- Check your pitch at a keyboard

Solmization

Singing with solfège syllables or scale degrees can help you understand the role that each pitch plays in a melody, and recognize recurring musical patterns. Several systems exist. Practice them all and then use the one your teacher prefers.

- In **movable-*do*** solfège, the home pitch of any melody is *do*.
- **Scale-degree** numbers are analogous to movable *do*.
- With **fixed *do***, C is always *do*; singing with **letter names** is analogous to fixed *do*.
- If your teacher prefers to sing using the system "*do* major/*la* minor" or with fixed *do*, use scale-degree numbers to identify musical patterns.

Treble and Bass Clefs

In *treble clef*, G4 is the second staff line. In *bass clef*, F3 is the fourth line.

Improvisation 1.1: Singing with Treble and Bass Clefs

Improvisation is the real-time creation and performance of new music.

1. *Point and Sing:*
   - Choose a system—solfège, numbers, or letters—and a clef.
   - Play C on a keyboard, point to it on the staff with the chosen clef, and then sing it using the system you chose.
   - Point to another note on the staff and sing it using the same system. Continue until you've made a satisfying melody.
   - *Strategies:*
     - Sing solfège syllables using pure vowels, like those in Spanish or Italian.
     - Sing "*sev*" for $\hat{7}$.
     - Check your pitch at the keyboard. Sing each note before playing it.

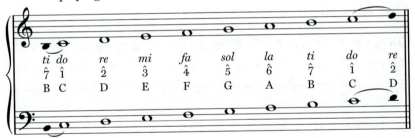

2. *Quick Composition:*

   Composition is music you create, capture, and save by notating or recording. Composition is often inspired by improvisation.
   - Perform Improvisation 1.1 until you improvise a melody you like.
   - Draw a clef and notate your melody, writing filled note heads for short durations and hollow note heads for long ones.

   Here is an example. Play C and sing it to hear whether you like yours better!

3. *Peer Evaluation:* Quick Composition Performances

Share your composition with others.

- Choose a pitch-mapping system—solfège, numbers, or letters—and play C.

- Ask one person to sing your composition, while others look at the music and listen.

- Evaluate the singer's pitch and solmization on a two-point scale: 2 is excellent, 1 is fair, 0 is weak.

Melodies

Play C, then sing each of the following stepwise melodies using solfège, numbers, or letters, as your teacher directs. Hold hollow note heads longer than filled ones.

1.8

Alto and Tenor Clefs

Movable C clefs associate C4 with a specific staff line. In *alto clef*, C4 is the middle line. In *tenor clef*, C4 is the fourth line.

Improvisation 1.2: Singing with Alto and Tenor Clefs

1. *Point and Sing:*

   - Choose a system—solfège, numbers, or letters—and a clef.
   - Play C on a keyboard, point to it on the chosen staff, and then sing it using the system you chose.
   - Point to another note on the staff and sing it using the same system. Continue until you've made a satisfying melody.

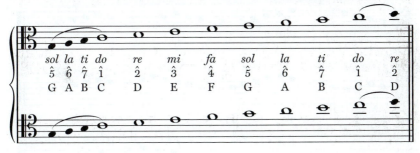

2. *Quick Composition:*

   - Perform Improvisation 1.2 until you improvise a melody you like.
   - Draw a clef and notate your melody, writing filled note heads for short durations and hollow note heads for long ones.

   Here are examples of notated improvisations, one in alto clef and one in tenor clef. Play C and sing each.

3. *Peer Evaluation:*

Share your composition with others.

- Choose a pitch-mapping system, and play C.
- Ask one person to sing your composition, while others look at the music and listen.
- Evaluate the singer's pitch and solmization on a two-point scale.

Melodies

Play C, then sing each of the following stepwise melodies using solfège, numbers, or letters, as your teacher directs. Hold hollow note heads longer than filled ones.

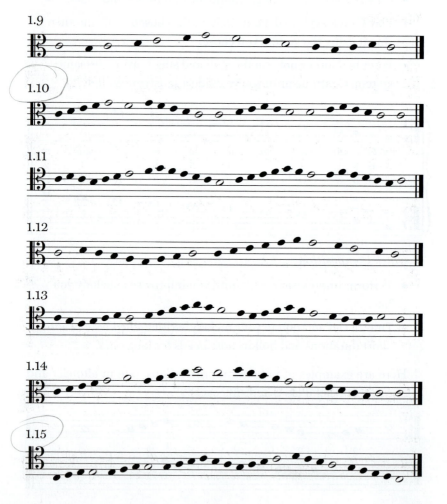

Singing Skips

Before singing a melody as notated, find each skip and practice it separately, like this.

Melodies

1.17

1.18

1.19

1.20

1.21

1.22

1.23

CHAPTER 2 Simple Meters

In this chapter you'll learn to:

- Conduct and perform simple duple, triple, and quadruple meters with a ♩ beat unit
- Apply rhythm-counting systems
- Evaluate melodic performances
- Transpose melodies using solfège and numbers
- Improvise and notate rhythms
- Perform music that begins with an anacrusis

Duple Meter

To perform duple meter:

- Choose a tempo you can maintain throughout.
- Conduct or tap as you perform. To conduct:
  - Move your right hand *down* for beat 1 and *up* for beat 2.
  - Make a small bounce on each beat.
- Perform *expressively*, observing dynamic markings and the relative stress of stronger and weaker beats.
- Sing with a neutral syllable like "ta" or with rhythm-counting syllables, as directed by your teacher.

Rhythms

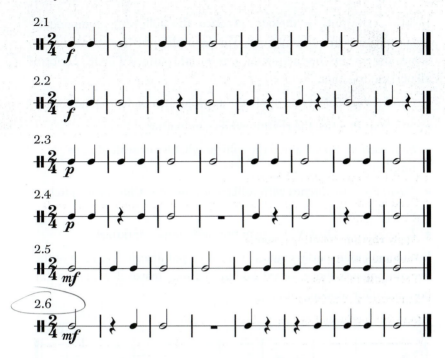

2.1

2.2

2.3

2.4

2.5

2.6

Rhythmic Duets

Perform with a partner. Switch parts and perform again.

Solo option: Conduct and perform one part aloud while tapping the other.

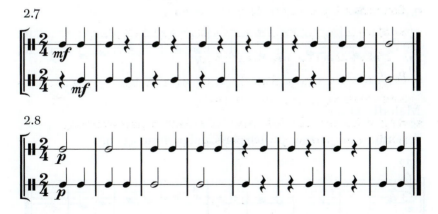

2.7

2.8

Melodies

Before performing a melody, practice the following components separately and in combinations. For example, practice speaking the solmization while conducting the appropriate pattern. Finally, perform all of them together.

- *Conducting:* Select and apply the appropriate conducting pattern.
- *Rhythm:* Practice the rhythm while conducting.
- *Solmization:* Speak aloud the solfège syllables or scale-degree numbers.
- *Pitch:* Sing the pitches with solfège or numbers. Check your pitch at the keyboard.
- *Expressivity:* Observe the dynamic and tempo markings.

Evaluate melodic performances using a 10-point scale. For each of the five components above, award 2 points for good to excellent; 1 point for fair; and 0 for weak or missing.

Melodic Duet

Perform with a partner. Switch parts and perform again.

Transposition Using Solfège and Scale-Degree Numbers

Melodies 2.13–2.18 appear twice, once beginning on C and once beginning on another pitch. Sing the melody on C. Then, using the same syllables or numbers, sing the melody beginning on the new pitch.

Melodies

2.13

2.17

2.18

Quadruple Meter

To conduct quadruple meter, move your right hand *down* for beat 1, *in* toward your heart for beat 2, *out* to the side for beat 3, and *up* for beat 4.

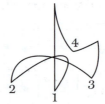

Improvisation 2.1:
Performing ○ Durations with ♩ Beat Units

Point and Sing: Point to a numbered pattern and perform it. While keeping a steady beat, point to another and perform. Continue until you can perform every pattern confidently.

Rhythms

2.19

2.20

2.21

2.22

Improvisation 2.2:
Performing Ties, Dots, and Syncopations

1. Perform patterns 1–5.

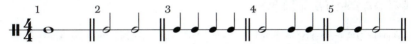

2. Perform (a), (b), and (c) to learn how adding ties to patterns 4, 5, and 3 creates three new patterns.

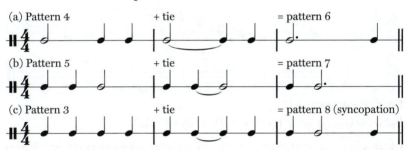

3. Drawing from patterns 1–8 improvise eight-measure segments.

4. *Quick Composition:* Notate your favorite rhythmic improvisation on a single staff. Indicate the meter signature, bar lines, and a specific tempo. Exchange your notated improvisation with a peer and perform each other's composition.

Rhythms

2.23

2.24

2.25

2.26

Melodies

Rests can substitute for notes of equal duration.

2.27

Allegretto

2.28

Andante

2.29

Moderato

Anacrusis

An anacrusis leads to a piece's first downbeat. Start the conducting pattern on the downbeat of the anacrusis measure, then begin performing aloud on the anacrusis note.

Rhythms

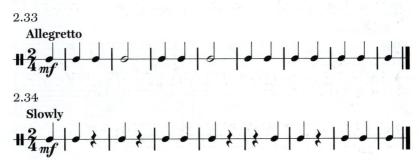

2.35

Allegro

2.36

Allegretto

Melodies

Sing *do* (1̂), the final pitch of each melody, and then sing up or down to find *sol* (5̂), the anacrusis.

2.37

Adagio

2.38

Allegretto

2.39

Allegro

2.40

Moderato

Duts

Duets

2.41

2.42

2.43

Triple Meter

To conduct triple meter, move your right hand *down* for beat 1, *out* for beat 2, and *up* for beat 3.

Improvisation 2.3:
Performing ♩. Durations with ♩ Beat Units

Point and sing: Point to a numbered pattern and perform it. While keeping a steady beat, point to another and perform. Continue until you can perform all patterns confidently. Drawing from all patterns, improvise eight-measure segments.

Rhythms

2.44

Allegretto

2.45

Moderato

2.46

Allegro

2.47

Fast

2.48

2.49

Duet

2.50

Keyboard 2.4: Reading and Identifying Pitches

1. Work in pairs. While one person plays each of the following notes on the keyboard, another checks for accuracy. Switch roles and perform again.

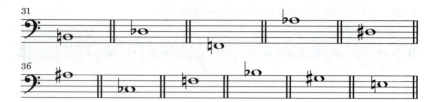

2. Using the pitches in exercise 1, play the pitch, then play a half step above and a half step below it. Then play a whole step above and below it. Ask a partner to check your work, then switch roles.

Melodies

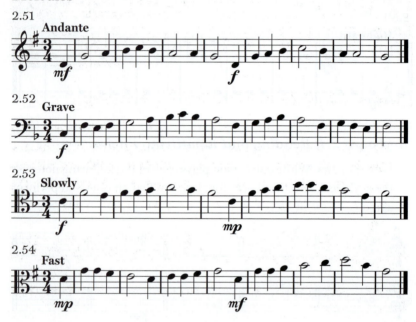

2.51 **Andante**

mf *f*

2.52 **Grave**

f

2.53 **Slowly**

f *mp*

2.54 **Fast**

mp *mf*

2.55 Béla Bartók, *Mikrokosmos*, Vol. 1, No. 2a

Sing the melody on C, but in a comfortable register.

♩ = 96

2.56 Traditional (United States), "Yankee Doodle"

Moderato

f

9

2.57 Traditional (England), "Hot Cross Buns"

Duet

2.58

Moderato

Keyboard 2.5: Performing Whole and Half Steps

1. Place your right-hand thumb on C4 (middle C). Play an ascending five-pitch white-key segment (ex. a), singing with letter names. Identify each adjacent pair as either a whole step (W) or a half step (H). Move your thumb up one white key (ex. b) and repeat the activity. Move up again (ex. c) and continue until you reach C5.

Variation: Place your left-hand little finger on C3 and double the right hand.

2. Choose a different starting pitch and change the whole- and half-step pattern to those shown in (a) and (b). While playing each new pattern, sing with letters, adding "sharp" or "flat" where needed.

(a) W-W-H-W   (b) W-H-W-W

CHAPTER 3

Beat Divisions, Pitch Collections, and Major Keys

In this chapter you'll learn to:

- Perform music with simple divisions of ♩ and ♩ beat units
- Sing melodies based on the major pentachord, major pentatonic scale, and major scale
- Improvise and compose rhythm patterns with simple divisions of ♩ and ♩ beat units

The Divided ♩ Beat Unit

Improvisation 3.1: Performing ♪ Beat Divisions

1. Conduct or tap in two while performing patterns 1–5.

2. Adding ties to patterns 4, 5, and 3 above creates patterns 6, 7, and 8.

Pattern #4 + a tie = #6   Pattern #5 + a tie = #7   Pattern #3 + a tie = #8

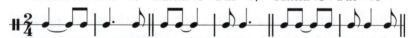

3. *Point and Sing:* Randomly point to a rhythm pattern and perform it. Keeping a steady beat, point to a new pattern and perform. Continue until you can perform all patterns confidently.

4. Drawing from the eight patterns above, improvise eight-measure segments.

5. *Quick Composition:* Notate your favorite improvisation on a single staff. Indicate the meter signature, bar lines, and a specific tempo.

6. *Perform:* Exchange your notated improvisation with a peer and perform each other's composition.

Simple Duple Rhythms

- Before performing, set a tempo you can maintain throughout.
- Conduct or tap lightly while performing.
- Perform expressively, giving attention to dynamics and the relative stress of stronger and weaker beats.
- Sing with counting syllables, or on a neutral syllable like "ta."

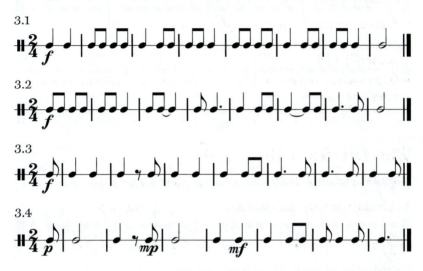

Simple Duple Rhythmic Duet

Sing with a partner, or tap one part while singing the other part aloud with counting syllables.

Simple Quadruple Rhythms

Simple Quadruple Rhythmic Duet

Simple Triple Rhythms

3.11

3.12

3.13

3.14

Simple Triple Rhythmic Duet

3.15

The Major Pentachord

Keyboard and Improvisation 3.2:
Performing Major Pentachords

1. At a keyboard, place your right- and left-hand fingers on the notes as shown. While playing the pitches, sing up and down with solfège, numbers, and letters. Between adjacent notes, W indicates a whole step and H a half step.

C major pentachord with right- and left-hand fingering

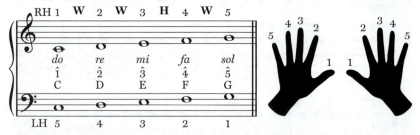

2. Beginning and ending on C, improvise short melodies with the C major pentachord. Sing the same notes you play, and use solfège, numbers, or letters. Don't worry about duration yet.

3. Beginning and ending on C, sing up and down the embellished major pentachord below with solfège, numbers, and letters. Then, improvise a melody, playing and singing pitches in an order you find pleasing. Generally, after singing *ti* ($\hat{7}$), rise to *do* ($\hat{1}$), and after *la* ($\hat{6}$), sing *sol* ($\hat{5}$).

Embellished C major pentachord (*ti–la*; $\hat{7}$-$\hat{6}$)

4. Beginning and ending on C, improvise again using the pitches of the embellished major pentachord above. This time choose from the two-beat rhythm patterns in 1–8.

5. *Quick Composition:* Notate your favorite improvisation. Write the clef (bass or treble), $\frac{2}{4}$ meter signature, and the pitch, rhythm, and all bar lines, including a final bar line in the last measure.

6. *Perform:* Exchange melodies with a partner. Play C and ask your partner to conduct in two while singing your melody with solfège, numbers, or letters. Then, swap roles and perform your partner's melody.

Melodies

3.16

3.17

3.18

3.19 Béla Bartók, No. 16 from *44 Duets*, Vol. I (adapted)

3.20

3.21 Traditional (Puerto Rico), *"Si me dan pasteles"* ("If You Give Me *Pasteles*")

3.22

3.23 Béla Bartók, No. 1 from *44 Duets*, Vol. I

3.24 Traditional (Europe), "Go Tell Aunt Rhody"

The Divided 𝅗𝅥 Beat Unit

Improvisation 3.3: Performing Rhythms in Cut Time

1. Conduct or tap two beats per measure while performing patterns 1–8.

2. *Point and Sing:* Point to a random rhythm pattern in exercise 1 and perform it. Keeping a steady beat, point to a new pattern and perform. Continue until you can perform all patterns confidently.

3. Drawing from patterns 1–8, improvise eight-measure segments.

4. Beginning and ending on C, improvise again. This time, include pitches from the embellished major pentachord, sung to your choice of the eight rhythm patterns from exercise 1.

Embellished C major pentachord (*ti-la*; $\hat{7}$-$\hat{6}$)

do	ti	do	re	mi	fa	sol	la	sol
$\hat{1}$	$\hat{7}$	$\hat{1}$	$\hat{2}$	$\hat{3}$	$\hat{4}$	$\hat{5}$	$\hat{6}$	$\hat{5}$
C	B	C	D	E	F	G	A	G

5. *Quick Composition:* Notate your favorite improvisation. Write the clef (bass or treble), meter signature (¢ or $\frac{2}{2}$), and the pitch, rhythm, and all bar lines, including a final bar line in the last measure.

6. *Perform:* Swap with a peer and sing each other's melody with solfège, numbers, or letters.

Rhythms

- Conduct or tap two beats per measure, keeping a steady tempo throughout.

- Perform expressively, observing dynamics and strong and weak beats.

- Sing with counting syllables, or on a neutral syllable like "ta."

3.25

3.26

3.27 Rhythms 3.27 and 3.28 are performed identically.

3.28

3.29

3.30

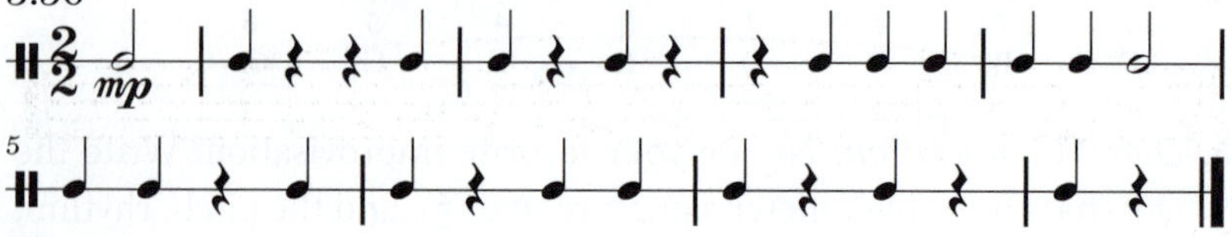

3.31

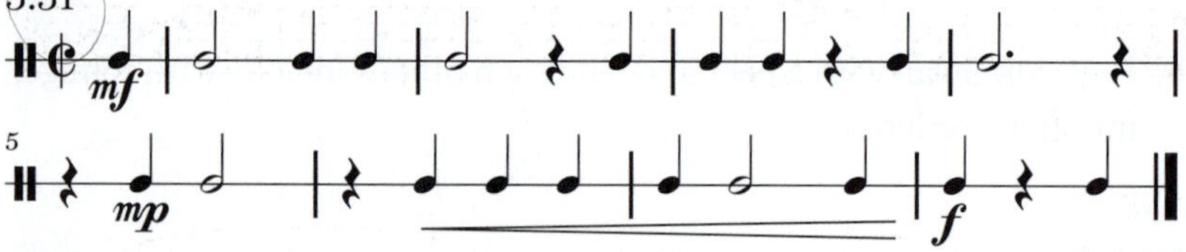

3.32

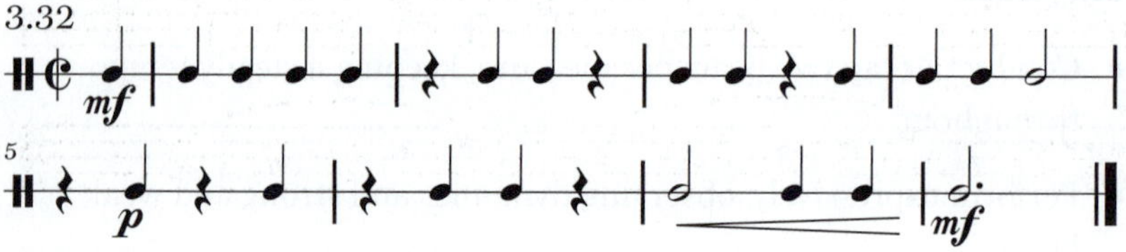

Duet

3.33

Melodies

3.34

3.35

3.36

3.37

3.38

Major Tetrachords and Major Scales

A major tetrachord is a W-W-H pattern, just like pitches 1–4 of a major pentachord. A major tetrachord on *do* ($\hat{1}$) and another on *sol* ($\hat{5}$) create a major scale.

Keyboard and Improvisation 3.4: Performing Major Scales

1. Place your fingers on the keyboard as shown. While playing, sing the scale with solfège and numbers.

C major scale = C major tetrachord + G major tetrachord

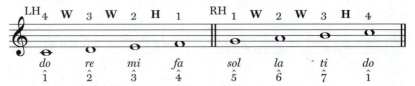

2. Beginning and ending on C, improvise a melody at the keyboard using notes from the C major scale. While playing, sing the same pitches with solfège or numbers.

3. Choose a different tonic pitch. From that pitch, create a major scale using two major tetrachords. Beginning and ending on the new *do* (1̂), improvise again at the keyboard. Each time you repeat the improvisation, begin with a new tonic pitch.

Melodies

3.39

3.40 Richard Rodgers, "Bye and Bye"

3.41

3.42

3.43 Traditional (Wales), "The Men of Harlech"

3.44 Gustav Mahler, Symphony No. 2, mvt. 1 (adapted)

3.45

3.46

3.47 Johnny Cash, "I Walk the Line"

The anacrusis consists of three quarter notes.

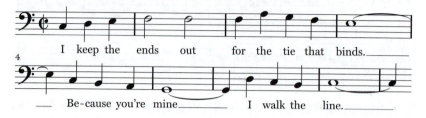

I keep the ends out for the tie that binds.

Be-cause you're mine I walk the line.

3.48

In rounds, performers follow a leader. When the leader reaches 2, the second performer begins at 1; when the leader reaches 3, the third performer begins at 1, and so on.

3.49 Henry Aldrich, "Great Tom Is Cast" (round in three parts)

3.50 Traditional (France), "Frère Jacques" (round in four parts)

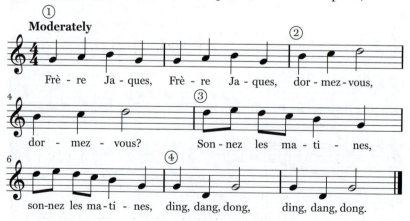

Frè - re Ja - ques, Frè - re Ja - ques, dor - mez - vous,

dor - mez - vous? Son - nez les ma - ti - nes,

son-nez les ma-ti - nes, ding, dang, dong, ding, dang, dong.

The Major Pentatonic Scale

A major pentatonic scale can be understood as a *do-do* ($\hat{1}$-$\hat{1}$) major scale that omits *fa* ($\hat{4}$) and *ti* ($\hat{7}$).

Keyboard and Improvisation 3.5: Performing Major Pentatonic Scales

1. Place your fingers on the keyboard as shown. While playing in tetrachords, sing all the pitches of the C major scale. Sing again, but omit *fa* ($\hat{4}$) and *ti* ($\hat{7}$) to create the C major pentatonic scale.

C major scale (all notes) and C major pentatonic scale (whole notes only)

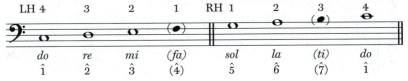

2. Beginning and ending on C, improvise a melody at the keyboard using notes of the C major pentatonic scale. While playing, sing the same pitches with solfège or numbers.

3. Choose a new tonic, then perform a major scale using two major tetrachords. Next, omit the notes *fa* ($\hat{4}$) and *ti* ($\hat{7}$) to perform a major pentatonic scale. Beginning and ending on the new *do* ($\hat{1}$), improvise another major pentatonic melody. Each time you repeat the improvisation, begin with a new tonic pitch.

Melodies

3.51

3.52 Traditional (England), "Mr. Frog Went A-Courting"

3.53

3.54 Mary Lantz, "The Drunkard's Doom" (adapted)

3.55

3.56

Compound Duple Meter

CHAPTER 4

In this chapter you'll learn to:

- Perform music in compound duple meter with the ♩. beat unit
- Sing major-key melodies in compound duple meter
- Improvise rhythms with compound divisions of the ♩. beat

⁶⁄₈ Meter: Fundamental Patterns

In ⁶⁄₈ the ♩. gets one beat that divides into three parts.

Improvisation 4.1: Performing ♩. Beats with Divisions

1. Conduct or tap in two while performing patterns 1–5. Sing aloud with counting syllables.

2. *Point and Sing:* While conducting or tapping in two, choose randomly among patterns 1–4 and improvise four- and eight-measure segments. End with pattern 5.

3. *Quick Composition:* Notate your favorite improvisation using only the patterns in exercise 1. Exchange with a peer. Conduct in two and perform your peer's rhythm aloud with counting syllables. Switch roles.

Rhythms

- Conduct in two or tap a tempo you can maintain throughout.
- Perform expressively, observing dynamics and stressing strong beats.
- Sing with counting syllables, or on a neutral syllable like "ta."

Part I Elements of Music

Rests do not alter beat divisions.

The next several rhythms feature an anacrusis.

Duets

Perform with a partner, or perform one part aloud while tapping the other. Switch parts and perform again.

4.19

Melodies

The next melodies are based on the major pentachord ($\hat{1}$–$\hat{5}$) or embellished major pentachord ($\hat{7}$–$\hat{6}$).

4.34

The next several melodies span an octave.

4.35

4.36

4.37

4.38

Part I Elements of Music

4.39

4.40

4.41 Traditional (France), *"Auprès de ma blonde"* ("Next to My Fair-Haired Lady")

In the following melodies, sing the final pitch, *do* ($\hat{1}$), then sing up the pentachord until you reach the starting pitch, *mi* or *sol* ($\hat{3}$ or $\hat{5}$).

4.42 Traditional (British Isles), "Oats, Peas, Beans"

Moderately fast

4.43 Traditional (England), "Three Blind Mice" (round in three parts)

Three blind mice,— Three blind mice,— see how they run,— see how they run,— They all ran af-ter the farm-er's wife, who cut off their tails with a carv-ing knife. Did you ev - er see such a sight in your life as three blind mice.—

4.44

mf   *mf*

4.45 Traditional (France), "*Vive l'amour*" ("Long Live Love")

Allegretto

mf   *f*

4.46

f   *mp*

4.47 Traditional (England), "Goodbye, My Lover, Goodbye"

4.48 Philip P. Bliss, "Wonderful Words of Life"

4.49 Ludwig van Beethoven, Sonatina in G Major, mvt. 2

4.50 Robert Schumann, *Album for the Young*, Op. 68, No. 18

CHAPTER 5

Minor Keys

In this chapter you'll learn to:

- Sing with chromatic solfège syllables and scale-degree numbers
- Sing minor-scale and minor-pentatonic melodies
- Perform and improvise subdivided beats in simple and compound meters

Chromatic Solfège Syllables and Scale-Degree Numbers

Keyboard 5.1: Performing Chromatic Pitches

Chromatic solfège and numbers use the major scale as their basis. A ♯ or ♭ placed before a scale degree means the pitch is raised or lowered a half step, respectively.

While playing, sing up and down the chromatic scale with solfège and numbers. Like other solfège syllables, the chromatic syllables should be sung with pure vowel sounds, as in Spanish or Italian.

Common Minor-Key Pitch Patterns

Keyboard and Improvisation 5.2:
Performing Minor-Key Pitch Patterns

A. Minor Pentachords and Tetrachords

1. While singing, play the C minor pentachord with both hands using the fingering provided.

C minor pentachord with right- and left-hand fingering

2. Play minor pentachords with both hands using the tonic pitches given. While playing, sing with solfège or numbers.

    C   G   E   A   D   B

3. The minor tetrachord is the first four notes of the minor pentachord. From each tonic in exercise A.2, play and sing a minor tetrachord.

B. Minor Scale Forms

1. While singing, play each of the following minor scales using the given fingering.

    (a) Natural minor (key-signature minor, descending melodic, or Aeolian mode)

    (b) Harmonic minor (use *ti* [$\hat{7}$] instead of *te* [$\flat\hat{7}$])

(c) Ascending melodic minor (use *la* [6̂] and *ti* [7̂] instead of *le* [♭6̂] and *te* [♭7̂])

2. From each pitch in exercise A.2, perform these minor-scale forms, up and down.

   (a) natural   (b) harmonic   (c) melodic minor

3. Select from these minor-key melodic segments to improvise melodies in $\frac{2}{4}$ or $\frac{6}{8}$. Use rhythm patterns consisting of beats and beat divisions.

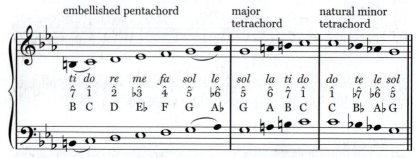

Strategies

- Embellished pentachord: Always move from *ti* to *do* (7̂–1̂) and *le* to *sol* (♭6̂–5̂).

- Major tetrachord: When *sol* rises to *la*, continue with *ti-do* (5̂–6̂–7̂–1̂).

- Natural minor tetrachord: When *do* falls to *te*, continue *le-sol* (1̂–♭7̂–♭6̂–5̂).

Examples

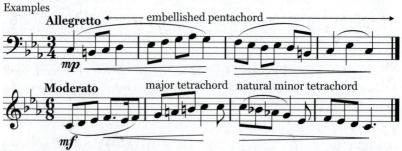

4. *Quick Composition:* Notate your favorite improvisation. Write a clef, and key and meter signatures. Beam notes to show beat grouping and include all bar lines. Exchange with a peer and sing each other's melody with solfège or numbers.

Melodies

5.1 Moderato

mp

5.2 Lively

mp   *mf*

5.3 Allegro

mf

5.4 Espressivo

mp

mf

5.5 Georg Philipp Telemann, Quartet in E Minor, mvt. 3

mf

The following examples are in melodic minor. When ascending from *sol* ($\hat{5}$), listen for *sol-la-ti-do* ($\hat{5}$-$\hat{6}$-$\hat{7}$-$\hat{1}$). When descending from *do* ($\hat{1}$), listen for *do-te-le-sol* ($\hat{1}$-♭$\hat{7}$-♭$\hat{6}$-$\hat{5}$).

5.6 Allegretto

f

The Subdivided ♩ Beat Unit

Improvisation 5.3: Performing Subdivided ♩ Beat Units

1. Conduct or tap in two while performing patterns 1–8. Sing aloud
   with counting syllables.

2. *Point and Sing:* Point to a pattern in exercise 1 and perform it. While keeping a steady beat, point to and perform a new pattern. Continue until you can perform all patterns accurately.

3. *Improvise:* With a partner or in a group, take turns improvising four-measure phrases based on patterns 1–8.

Rhythms

5.11

Adding a tie to a beat pattern can create a new pattern.

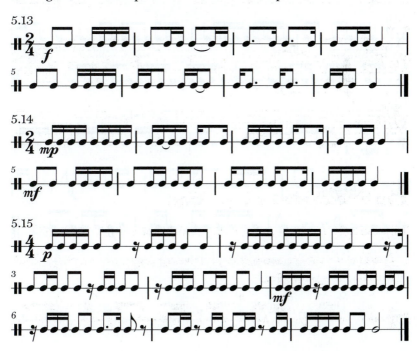

5.16

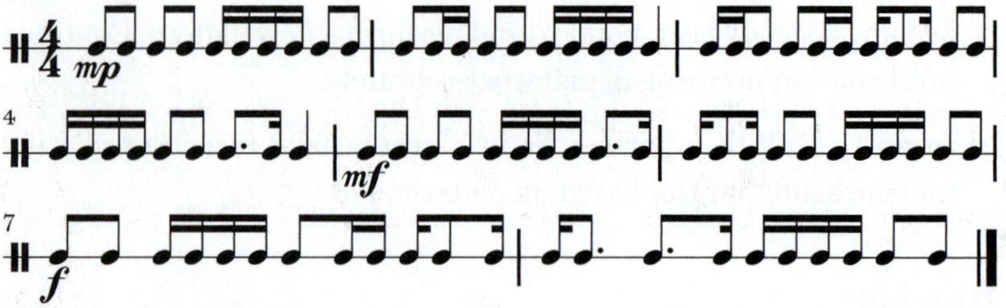

5.17

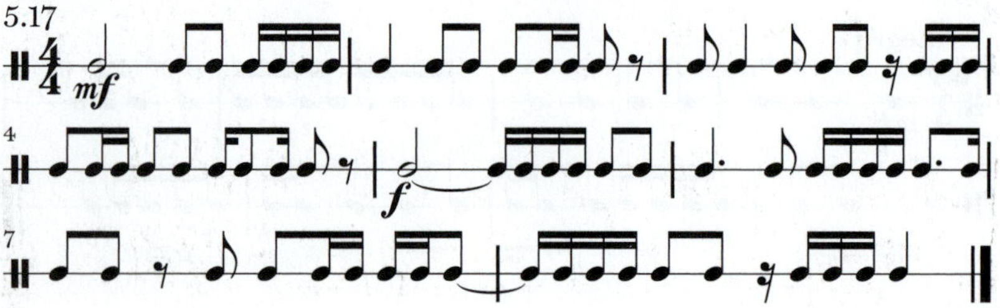

5.18

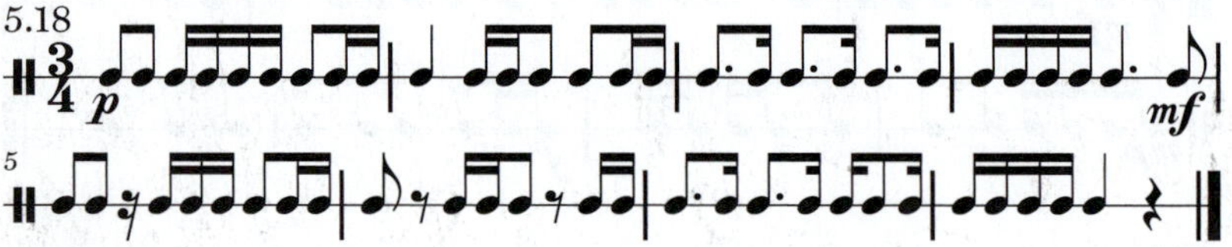

5.19

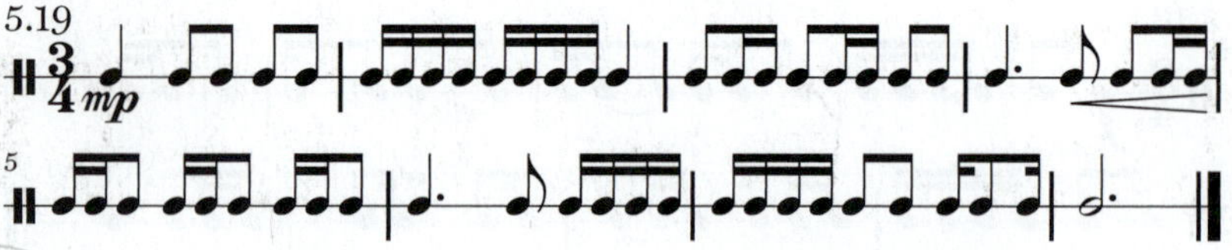

5.20

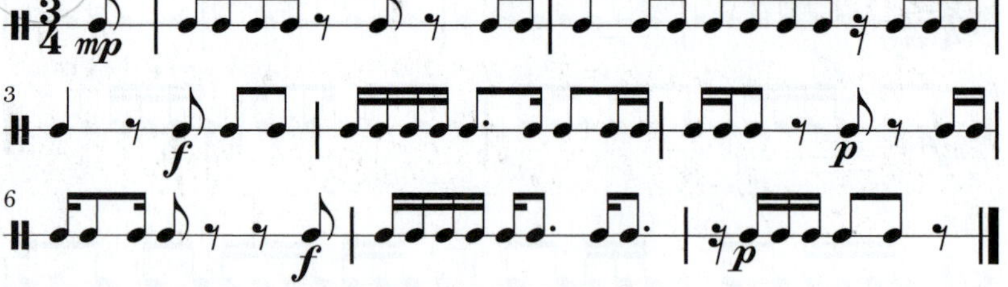

Duets

5.21

Melodies

5.23 Joseph Haydn, String Quartet in G Minor, Op. 74, No. 3, mvt. 2

5.24 Ludwig van Beethoven, Agnus Dei, from *Mass in C*, Op. 86

5.25 Traditional (Hebrew), *"Zum Gali Gali"* ("To Galilee")

5.26 Johannes Brahms, Intermezzo in C♯ Minor, Op. 117, No. 3 (adapted)

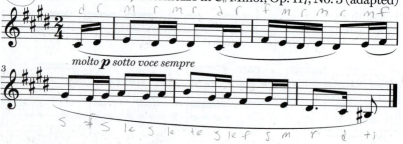

5.27 Traditional (France), "Pat-a-Pan"

5.28

5.29 Clara Schumann, *Le Ballet des Revenants* (adapted)

5.30

5.31

5.32

5.33

Note that in this melody the augmented second occurs between *le* and *ti* (♭6̂ and ♯7̂).

5.34 Traditional (England), "Ah, Poor Bird" (round in 3 parts)

The Subdivided ♩. Beat Unit

Improvisation 5.4: Performing Subdivided ♩. Beat Units

1. Conduct or tap in two while performing patterns 1–7. Sing aloud with counting syllables.

2. *Point and Sing:* Point to a pattern and perform it. While keeping a steady beat, point to and perform a new pattern. Continue until you can perform all patterns accurately.

3. *Improvise:* With a partner or in a group, take turns improvising four-measure phrases based on patterns 1–7.

Rhythms

Adding a tie to a beat pattern can create a new pattern.

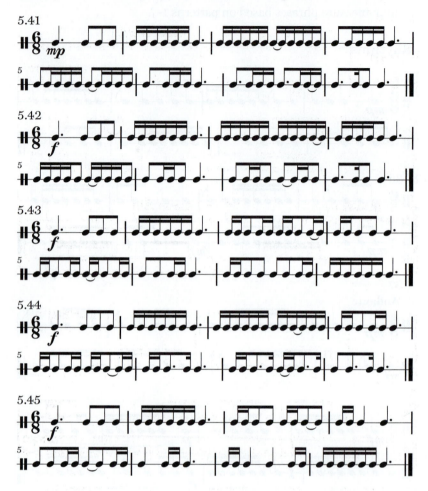

Duets

5.46

Melodies

5.48

5.49 Emilie Zumsteeg, "*Romanze*" No. 4, from *Fünf Lieder mit Gegleitung der Guitarre*

5.50 Giacomo Meyerbeer, "*De ma première amie*" ("Of My First Beloved")

5.51

5.52

5.53

5.54

The Minor Pentatonic Scale

Compared with natural minor, minor pentatonic omits *re* ($\hat{2}$) and *le* ($\flat\hat{6}$).

Keyboard and Improvisation 5.5: Performing Minor Pentatonic Scales

1. Play and sing the C natural minor and minor pentatonic scales.

2. For each given pitch, perform natural minor, then minor pentatonic up and down.

   C D G A E B

3. Choose $\frac{2}{4}$ or $\frac{6}{8}$. Conduct or tap in two with a steady beat. Sing notes from the minor pentatonic scale using a mix of beats, beat divisions, and beat subdivisions. Begin and end with *do* ($\hat{1}$).

Melodies

5.55

CHAPTER 6

Intervals, Compound Quadruple, and Compound Triple Meter

In this chapter you'll learn to:

- Perform intervals within études and melodies from literature
- Improvise rhythms with both simple and compound divisions of the beat
- Perform compound melodies
- Perform music in compound quadruple and compound triple meters with a ♩. beat unit

Major, Minor, and Perfect Intervals above and below a Given Pitch

Keyboard and Improvisation 6.1:
Performing Major, Minor, and Perfect Intervals

A. Intervals from the Major Scale

1. While playing, sing each interval above and below C with solfège, numbers, letters, and interval names as shown. For example: "*do-do*, î-î, C-C, perfect unison"; "*do-re*, î-2̂, C-D, major second"; etc. Improvise the rhythms using only simple beat divisions and subdivisions.

C major scale: Major and perfect intervals *above* C

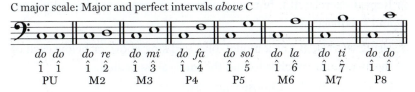

do do	*do re*	*do mi*	*do fa*	*do sol*	*do la*	*do ti*	*do do*
î î	î 2̂	î 3̂	î 4̂	î 5̂	î 6̂	î 7̂	î î
PU	M2	M3	P4	P5	M6	M7	P8

C major scale: Minor and perfect intervals *below* C

do do	*do ti*	*do la*	*do sol*	*do fa*	*do mi*	*do re*	*do do*
î î	î 7̂	î 6̂	î 5̂	î 4̂	î 3̂	î 2̂	î î
PU	m2	m3	P4	P5	m6	m7	P8

2. Repeat exercise A.1, but improvise using compound beat divisions and subdivisions.

3. Using exercise A.1 as a model, play and sing above or below each of the given tonic pitches to find the intervals specified.

   C G F D B♭ Choose your own!

   • Play the following intervals *above* the given tonic pitches:
     M3, P5, M2, M6, P4, and M7

   • Play the following intervals *below* the given tonic pitches:
     m2, m6, P4, m3, m7, and P5

B. Intervals from the Phrygian Mode (Natural Minor with ♭2̂)

1. Lower major-scale degrees 2̂, 3̂, 6̂, and 7̂ one half step to produce the Phrygian mode. While playing, sing with solfège, numbers, letters, and interval names as shown. Improvise the rhythm using only simple beat divisions and subdivisions.

C Phrygian mode: Minor and perfect intervals *above* C

do do	do ra	do me	do fa	do sol	do le	do te	do do
1̂ 1̂	1̂ ♭2̂	1̂ ♭3̂	1̂ 4̂	1̂ 5̂	1̂ ♭6̂	1̂ ♭7̂	1̂ 1̂
PU	m2	m3	P4	P5	m6	m7	P8

C Phrygian mode: Major and perfect intervals *below* C

do do	do te	do le	do sol	do fa	do me	do ra	do do
1̂ 1̂	1̂ ♭7̂	1̂ ♭6̂	1̂ 5̂	1̂ 4̂	1̂ ♭3̂	1̂ ♭2̂	1̂ 1̂
PU	M2	M3	P4	P5	M6	M7	P8

2. Repeat exercise B.1, but improvise using compound beat divisions and subdivisions.

3. Using exercise B.1 as a model, play and sing above or below each of the given tonic pitches to find the intervals specified.

   C G A B E Choose your own!

   • Play the following intervals *above* the given tonic pitches:
     m3, P5, m2, m6, P4, and m7

   • Play the following intervals *below* the given tonic pitches:
     M2, M6, P4, M3, M7, and P5

C. Ascending and Descending Major, Minor, and Perfect Intervals

Using the exercises in A.1 and B.1 as a model, play and sing above or below each of the given tonic pitches to find the intervals specified.

C   A   E♭   Choose your own!

- Play the following intervals *above* the given tonic pitches: M2, M7, m2, m7, M3, P5, and P4

- Play the following intervals *below* the given tonic pitches: m2, m7, M3, P5, P4, m6, and M7

Interval Études and Compound Melody

Sometimes skips and leaps within a single melody can imply two or more lines that tend to move by step in their own register, a technique called *compound melody.*

Melodies

When rehearsing compound melodies, sing each implied line separately, then sing the melody as written.

6.1 Intervals above and below the tonic in the major scale

6.2 Intervals above and below the tonic in the natural minor scale

6.3 Intervals above and below the tonic in the melodic minor scale

6.4 Major-key thirds

6.5 Minor-key thirds

6.6 Major-key fourths

6.7 Minor-key fourths

6.8 Major-key fifths

6.9 Minor-key fifths

6.10

6.11

6.12

6.13

Compound Quadruple Meter

Compound quadruple's four ♩. beats each divide into three parts.

Rhythms

Because two compound duple measures make one measure of compound quadruple, the former has twice as many downbeats. When performing 6.14a–b and 6.15a–b, conduct the $\frac{6}{8}$ meter in two and the $\frac{12}{8}$ meter in four.

6.14a
Allegretto

6.14b
Allegretto

6.18

6.19

6.20

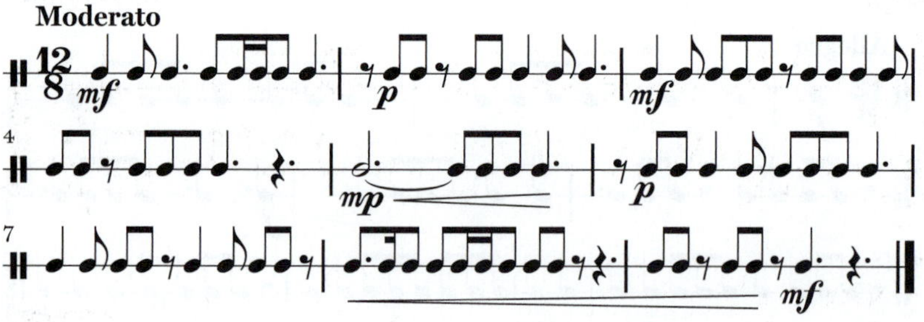

6.21

6.22

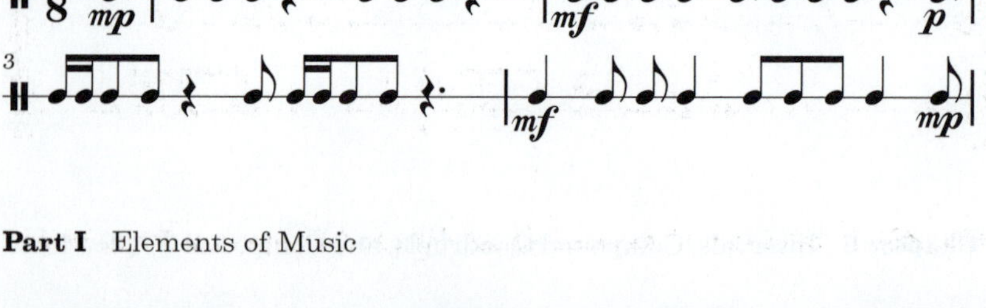

Duets

Perform with a partner. Switch parts and perform again.

Solo option: Conduct and perform one part aloud while tapping the other.

6.23

Andante

6.24

Allegretto

Compound Triple Meter

Compound triple meter's three ♩. beats each divide into three parts.

Rhythms

Conduct in three when performing compound triple meter.

6.25

Slowly

6.26

Allegro

6.27

Allegro

6.28

Allegretto

6.29

6.30

6.31

Duets

6.32

6.33

Compound Duple, Triple, and Quadruple Meters in Context

Melodies

6.34 Charles Gounod, *"Où voulez-vous aller?"* ("Where Do You Want to Go?") (adapted)

6.35 Thomas Arne, "A-Hunting We Will Go"

6.36 Fanny Mendelssohn Hensel, "*Schwanenlied*"
("Swan Song") (adapted)

6.37 Traditional (Ireland), "The Haymaker's Jig"

6.38 Traditional (Ireland), "The Newly Married Couple"

6.39 Johann Sebastian Bach, Chorale: *"Jesus bleibet meine Freude"* ("Jesu, Joy of Man's Desiring"), from Cantata No. 147 (adapted)

6.40 Johann Sebastian Bach, Violin Concerto No. 1 in A Minor, mvt. 3 (adapted)

6.41 George Frideric Handel, Harpsichord Suite in G Major, Gigue

6.42 Traditional (England), "Beaux of London City"

6.43 Traditional (United States), "The House of the Rising Sun"

6.44 Traditional (Germany), *"O wie wohl ist mir am Abend"* ("Oh, How Lovely Is the Evening") (round in three parts)

Augmented and Diminished Intervals

Keyboard 6.2: Performing Augmented and Diminished Intervals

A. Augmented Intervals

Change the given perfect and major intervals to augmented intervals.

1. Play the given interval, then raise the upper pitch a half step and play again; name the new interval.

2. Play the given interval again, then lower the bottom pitch a half step and play again; name the new interval.

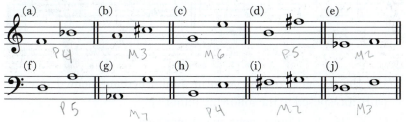

B. Diminished Intervals

Change the following perfect and minor intervals to diminished intervals.

1. Play the given interval, then lower the upper pitch a half step and play again; name the new interval.

2. Play the given interval again, then raise the bottom pitch a half step and play again; name the new interval.

C. Resolving Diminished and Augmented Intervals

Diminished/augmented interval pairs and their resolutions often occur between particular scale degrees. Diminished intervals contract, while augmented intervals expand.

1. Each interval pair appears harmonically, then as a compound melody. Play up-stem notes with your right hand and down-stem notes with the left. While playing both parts, sing the lower part. Play again and sing the upper part.

2. Use the model above to perform diminished/augmented interval pairs transposed to the following minor keys.

    C   A   G   E   Choose your own minor key!

CHAPTER 7

Triads and Half-Note Beat Units

In this chapter you'll learn to:

- Perform and improvise major, minor, diminished, and augmented triads
- Perform music that features major- and minor-key triads
- Perform simple-meter music with ♩ beat units

Major and Minor Triads

Keyboard and Improvisation 7.1:
Performing Major and Minor Triads

A. Performing Major and Minor Pentachords and Triads

1. Choose a tonic pitch, beat grouping (duple, triple, or quadruple), and beat division (simple or compound). Starting on the tonic, improvise a melody that includes a major pentachord and triad, then a minor pentachord and triad. While playing, sing with solfège or numbers.

Examples

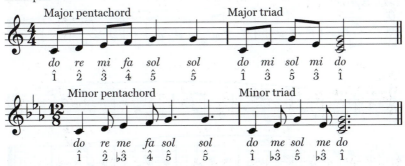

2. Choose a new tonic and repeat the improvisation. For each new tonic, vary both the meter and the rhythm patterns.

B. Performing Major- and Minor-Scale Triads

1. Choose a tonic pitch for a major key and perform a triad on every step of the ascending major scale. See the following model for an example of rhythmic interpretation and how to voice the triads. Repeat the exercise from high *do* (1̂), descending by step until reaching the tonic again.

Example: C major scale triads

2. Choose a tonic pitch for a minor key and perform a triad on every step of the ascending scale. Use key-signature pitches, but use *ti* (7̂) in triads built on 5̂ and 7̂. When descending from high *do* (1̂), use only pitches from natural minor.

Melodies

Exercises 7.1–7.4 appear in parallel major (a) and minor (b) keys. Compare the quality of their triads.

7.1a

mp

7

7.1b

mf

7

7.5 Traditional (United States), "The Dear Companion"

7.6 Traditional (Germany), "*Quem Pastores Laudavere*"
("Whom Shepherds Praise")

7.7 Traditional (American spiritual), "Rock of My Soul"

7.8 Traditional (American spiritual), "Come Along, Moses"

Simple Meter with Divided ♩ Beats

Improvisation 7.2: Performing ♩ Beats with ♪ Divisions

1. *Point and Sing:* Conduct or tap in two and perform patterns 1–8.
   Then, point to a random pattern and perform it. Keeping a steady
   beat, point to a new pattern and perform. Continue until you can
   perform all patterns accurately.

2. *Quick Composition:* Notate your favorite improvisation using
   patterns 1–8. Exchange with a peer. Conduct in two and perform
   your peer's rhythm aloud with counting syllables.

Rhythms

For comparison, perform rhythms 7.9a and 7.9b, which sound the same.

7.9a
Andante

7.9b
Andante

7.10

Duets

7.18

7.19

7.20

7.21

7.22

Melodies

7.23

7.24

7.25

7.26 Donovan, "Brother Sun, Sister Moon"

7.27 Ted Daffan, "Born to Lose"

7.28 Jerome Kern, "Look for the Silver Lining"

7.29 Béla Bartók, No. 2 from *44 Duets*, Vol. I (adapted)

7.30 Gene Autry, "Back in the Saddle Again"

7.31 A. Emmett Adams, "The Bells of St. Mary's"

7.32 Traditional (American spiritual), "Oh Brothers, Don't Get Weary"

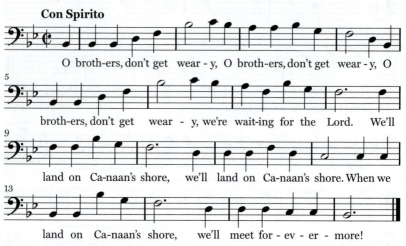

Con Spirito

O broth-ers, don't get wear - y, O broth-ers, don't get wear - y, O broth-ers, don't get wear - y, we're wait-ing for the Lord. We'll land on Ca-naan's shore, we'll land on Ca-naan's shore. When we land on Ca-naan's shore, we'll meet for - ev - er - more!

7.33 Louis Bourgeois, "Old Hundredth" (adapted)

Moderato

7.34 Traditional (Denmark), "Ribold and Guldborg"

7.35 Martin Luther, *Ein feste Burg* ("A Mighty Fortress," adapted by Michael Praetorius)

7.36 William Byrd, Galliard to the First Pavan, from *My Lady Nevell's Book*

7.37

7.38 Tomás Luis de Victoria, "*O regem cæli*" ("O, King of Heaven," adapted)

The tonic pitch of this melody is F.

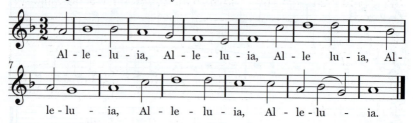

Al - le - lu - ia,   Al - le - lu - ia,   Al - le   lu - ia,   Al -
le - lu - ia,   Al - le - lu - ia,   Al - le - lu - ia.

7.39 Johann Schein, Gagliarda, from *Banchetto musicale*,
Suite No. 10 (adapted)

7.40 Traditional (England), "*Deo Gratias*"

Moderato

f Our   King   went   forth   to   Nor - mand - y   with
grace___   and   might___   of___   chiv - al - ry.

7.41 Francisco Guerrero, "*A un niño llorando*" ("To a Crying Child"),
from *Canciones y villanescas espirituales* (adapted)

Duet

7.42 Traditional (Germany), *"Ad cantus laetitiae"* ("The Joy of Singing") *Sight*

Augmented and Diminished Triads

Keyboard and Improvisation 7.3:
Performing Augmented and Diminished Triads

1. Choose a pitch and perform a major triad. Then, raise the fifth one half step to create an augmented triad. Repeat the exercise several times, each time with a new tonic.

2. Choose a pitch and perform a minor triad. Then, *lower* the fifth one half step to create a diminished triad. Repeat the exercise several times, each time with a new tonic.

3. In minor keys, the triads on the supertonic (m. 2 in the model) and leading tone (m. 4) are both diminished. Play tonic pitch D and sing the model to hear the d5 interval resolve inward to a third. Choose a new tonic pitch and perform the model again. For each new tonic, vary the meter and rhythm.

Model: Tonic pitch D

CHAPTER 8

Seventh Chords, Dotted-Half-Note Beat Units, and Disruptions of the Pulse

In this chapter you'll learn to:

- Improvise arpeggiations of the Mm7, the MM7, and the mm7
- Perform études that isolate seventh chords in major and minor keys
- Perform in compound meter with dotted-half-note beat units
- Perform disruptions of the pulse

Seventh Chords

Add a seventh to a triad to create one of these five seventh chords.

Triad quality +	7th quality =	Seventh chord	or lead-sheet symbol(s)
M	M	MM7	maj7, ma7, M7, ∆7
M	m	Mm7	7
m	m	mm7	min7, mi7, −7
d	m	dm7	ø7, min7(♭5), mi7(♭5), m7(♭5)
d	d	dd7	°7, dim7

Keyboard 8.1: Performing Seventh Chords from a Given Root

1. Play a B major triad. Double its root at the octave. Then, lower one chord tone at a time to play each type of seventh chord.

Example: The root is B.

2. Perform the exercise again from roots E, A, C, F, and G.

Improvisation 8.2: Performing Melodies That Outline the Mm7, MM7, and mm7

1. Select a major key and, from the choices provided, a rhythm and a seventh chord. Then, use the rhythm and seventh chord to improvise a melody, ending on *do* (1̂). Sing "*sev*" for 7̂.

Rhythm Choices

Seventh Chord Choices

Mm7 expressed as *sol-ti-re-fa* (5̂-7̂-2̂-4̂)

MM7 expressed as *do-mi-sol-ti* (1̂-3̂-5̂-7̂)

mm7 expressed as *re-fa-la-do* (2̂-4̂-6̂-1̂)

Sample solution in C major using the March rhythm and a MM7

2. *Quick Composition:* Notate your favorite improvisation. Exchange with a peer and sing each other's melody with solfège or numbers.

Melodies

8.1 Major-key seventh chords

8.2 Minor-key seventh chords

8.3 Major-key seventh chords

8.4 Minor-key seventh chords

8.5 Traditional (Hawai'i), *Ua Hiki No Me Au* ("'Tis Well with Me")

8.6 Traditional (Germany), *"Unterländers Heimweh"*
("Lowlander's Homesickness")

Moderately

8.7 Maria Agata Szymanowska, *"Caprice sur la romance de Joconde"*
("Caprice on the Romance of Mona Lisa") (adapted)

Andante

8.8 Traditional (Germany), *"Des Buben Herzleid"*
("The Boy's Heartache")

Andante

Compound Meter with Divided 𝅗𝅥. Beats

Improvisation 8.3: Performing 𝅗𝅥. Melodies with Beat Divisions

1. Conduct or tap in two while performing patterns 1-5. Sing aloud with counting syllables.

2. *Point and Sing:* While conducting or tapping in two, choose randomly among patterns 1-4 and improvise four- and eight-measure segments. End with pattern 5.

3. *Quick Composition:* Notate your favorite improvisation. Exchange with a peer. Conduct in two and perform your peer's improvisation aloud.

Rhythms

Conduct the next several rhythms with a two-beat pattern. Compare rhythms 8.9a–b, and 8.10a–b, which sound the same.

8.9a

8.9b

Conduct $\frac{12}{4}$ meter with a four-beat pattern.

8.15

8.16

8.17

Conduct $\frac{9}{4}$ meter with a three-beat pattern.

8.18

8.19

8.20

Duets

8.21

8.22

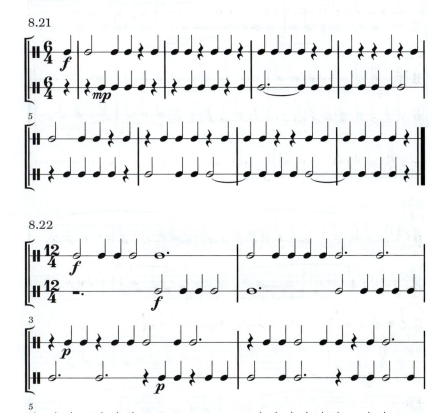

8.23

Melodies

8.24

8.25

8.26 Traditional (United Kingdom), "Cotillion" (adapted)

Allegretto

8.27

8.28

8.29 Traditional (Netherlands), *"Na Ostland vil ik varen"*
("To the East Will I Wander")

8.30

8.31 Traditional (Ireland), "Planks of Connaught"

8.32 John Stafford Smith and Ralph Tomlinson,
"The Anacreontic Song" (adapted)

To A - na - creon in Heav'n where he sat in full glee, A
few songs of har - mo - ny sent a pe - ti - tion, That
he their in - spi - rer and pa - tron would be, When this
an - swer ar - riv'd from the jol - ly old Gre - cian.

In 1814 Francis Scott Key set his poem "The Star-Spangled Banner" to Stafford's melody. In 1931 Key's setting became the U.S. national anthem.

8.33 Traditional (Germany), *Altes Minnelied* ("Old Love Song")

8.34

8.35

8.36 Traditional (England), "Old Chisholm Trail" (adapted)

Andante

mf Come a-long boys and lis - ten to my tale, I'll

tell you of my trou-bles on the old Chis-holm Trail. Come a

ti yi yip - py, yip - py yea, yip - py yea, Come a

ti yi yip - py, yip - py yea.

8.37 Traditional (England), "Lydia Pinkham" (adapted)

Liltingly

8.38

8.39

8.40 Traditional (Ireland), "Buttermilk and Pratties"

Disruptions of the Pulse

Several symbols and terms indicate disruptions of the pulse.

⌢	*Fermata*: Hold a note longer than its rhythmic value.
'	Breath mark: Take a breath.
// and **G.P.**	*Caesura* and grand pause: Stop the pulse temporarily.
rit. and *rall.*	*Ritardando* and *rallentando*: Gradually slow down.
accel.	*Accelerando*: Gradually speed up.
a tempo	*A tempo*: Resume the original tempo.

Rhythms

As you conduct, practice leading into and out of each disruption and gracefully returning to the original tempo.

CHAPTER 9

The Diatonic Modes, Counterpoint, and Borrowed Beat Divisions in Simple Meter

In this chapter you'll learn to:

- Perform solo *cantus firmi* in movable C, treble, and bass clefs
- Improvise note-to-note contrapuntal melodies against a given *cantus firmus*
- Perform modern modal melodies
- Perform borrowed beat divisions in simple meter (triplets)

The Diatonic Modes

The major scale is also called the Ionian mode and natural minor the Aeolian. Other modes may be understood as rotations of the major scale.

Keyboard and Improvisation 9.1: Performing Diatonic Modes

1. Play and sing each mode using both of these strategies.

Parallel syllables	Relative syllables
Call a mode's tonic *do* (1̂) and use chromatic solfège and numbers.	Imagine a mode to be a rotation of a major scale and us the major-scale solfège syllables and numbers.

(a) Dorian mode

Perform a natural minor scale and raise ♭6 a half step.

Call the first pitch *re* (2̂). Perform a major scale from *re* to *re* (2̂-2̂).

do	re	me	fa	sol	la	te	do		re	mi	fa	sol	la	ti	do	re
1̂	2̂	♭3̂	4̂	5̂	6̂	♭7̂	1̂		2̂	3̂	4̂	5̂	6̂	7̂	1̂	2̂

(b) Phyrgian mode

Perform a natural minor scale and lower 2̂ a half step (sung *ra*).

Call the first pitch *mi* (3̂). Perform a major scale from *mi* to *mi* (3̂-3̂).

do	ra	me	fa	sol	le	te	do		mi	fa	sol	la	ti	do	re	mi
1̂	♭2̂	♭3̂	4̂	5̂	♭6̂	♭7̂	1̂		3̂	4̂	5̂	6̂	7̂	1̂	2̂	3̂

(c) Lydian mode

Perform a major scale and raise 4̂ a half step (sung *fi*).

Call the first pitch *fa* (4̂). Perform a major scale from *fa* to *fa* (4̂-4̂).

do	re	mi	fi	sol	la	ti	do		fa	sol	la	ti	do	re	mi	fa
1̂	2̂	3̂	♯4̂	5̂	6̂	7̂	1̂		4̂	5̂	6̂	7̂	1̂	2̂	3̂	4̂

(d) Mixolydian mode

Perform a major scale and lower 7̂ a half step (sung *te*).

Call the first pitch *sol* (5̂). Perform a major scale from *sol* to *sol* (5̂-5̂).

do	re	mi	fa	sol	la	te	do		sol	la	ti	do	re	mi	fa	sol
1̂	2̂	3̂	4̂	5̂	6̂	♭7̂	1̂		5̂	6̂	7̂	1̂	2̂	3̂	4̂	5̂

2. Beginning on the given pitch, play up and down the mode specified. While playing, sing with solfège or numbers using each strategy above.

D Dorian	F Mixolydian	G♯ Aeolian
B Phrygian	B♭ Lydian	F Phrygian
A Lydian	D♭ Mixolydian	E Lydian
G Mixolydian	B Ionian	E Dorian

3. Choose a mode and improvise a melody that begins and ends on its final. Ask a peer to listen while you perform and to identify the mode you sang.

Cantus Firmi

A *cantus firmus* (CF; plural, *cantus firmi*) is a modal melody on which contrapuntal music may be based.

Melodies

9.1 Johann Joseph Fux

9.2 Thomas Morley

9.3 Johann Joseph Fux

9.4 Anatoly Layadov

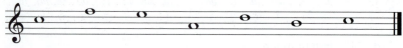

9.5 Johann Joseph Fux

Note-to-Note (1:1) Counterpoint

Keyboard and Improvisation 9.2:
Performing a CF and Its Counterpoint

1. Play and sing each CF beginning, middle, and ending.

2. Play the CF while singing each of its five possible counterpoints.

3. Choose a beginning, a middle, and an ending to create your own CF melody.

4. Play your CF while singing its counterpoint.

5. *Quick Composition:* Notate your favorite improvisation. Exchange with a peer and sing each other's counterpoint with solfège, numbers, or letters.

Duets

CF melodies 9.1-9.5 are given, now with a counterpoint (CPT). Play one part while singing the other, or sing with a partner.

9.6 Johann Joseph Fux

9.7 Thomas Morley

9.8 Johann Joseph Fux

9.9 Anatoly Layadov

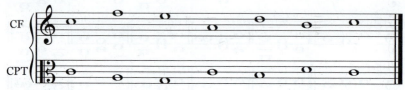

9.10 Johann Joseph Fux

9.11 Anonymous, 16th century, *"Gaudete"* ("Rejoice")

Modal Melodies

Sing these modal melodies using the same strategies as with *cantus firmi*.

Dorian

9.12

9.13 Béla Bartók, No. 18 from *44 Duets*, Vol. I (adapted)

9.14 Traditional (England), "The Drunken Sailor"

9.15

Phrygian

9.16

9.17

9.18

9.19 Béla Bartók, No. 6 from *44 Duets*, Vol. I (adapted)

The final of this mode is B.

Lydian

9.20

9.21

9.22

9.23 Edvard Grieg, "*Jon Vestafes Springdans*" ("Jon Vestafe's Springar"), *Norwegian Peasant Dance*s, Op. 72, No. 2 (adapted)

Allegro Moderato

Mixolydian

9.24

9.25

9.26

9.27 Traditional (United States), "Old Joe Clark"

Old Joe Clark   had   a house   fif-teen sto-ries   high   and

ev'-ry   sto-ry   in that house was   filled with chick-en   pie!

Fare thee well,___   Old Joe Clark,   fare thee well, I   say;

fare thee well,___   Old Joe Clark, I   best be on my   way.

Aeolian

9.28

9.29 Traditional (United States), "All the Pretty Horses"

Moderato

Sometimes, Aeolian melodies omit $\hat{6}$.

9.30 Traditional (Canada), "Land of the Silver Birch"

Land of the sil-ver birch, home of the beav-er, where still the

might-y moose wan-ders at will. Blue lake and rock-y shore

I will re - turn once more. Boom did-dy boom boom

boom did-dy boom boom boom did-dy boom boom boom!

9.31 Thomas Casey and Charles Connolly, "Drill, Ye Tarriers, Drill"

Ensembles

9.32 Traditional (Hebrew folk song), *"Shalom, Chaverim"* ("Peace, Friends") (round in three parts)

9.33 Traditional (England), "Hey, Ho, Anybody Home?" (round in three parts)

Borrowed Beat Divisions in Simple Meter (Triplets)

Borrowed beat divisions occur when a compound-meter beat division appears in simple meter, or vice versa.

♪ Triplets

An eighth-note triplet equals the duration of a quarter note.

Improvisation 9.3: Performing ♪ Triplets

1. Conduct or tap in two while performing patterns 1–9.

2. *Point and Sing:* Point to a rhythm pattern and perform it. Keeping a steady beat, point to a new pattern and perform. Continue until you can perform all patterns accurately. Improvise eight-measure segments.

3. *Quick Composition:* Notate your favorite improvisation using patterns
   1–9. Exchange with a peer. Conduct in two and perform your peer's
   rhythm aloud with counting syllables.

Rhythms

Duets

Melodies

9.43 **Tempo giusto**

9.44 Edvard Grieg, "Spring Dance," No. 3 from *Six Norwegian Mountain Melodies* (adapted)

Allegro con brio

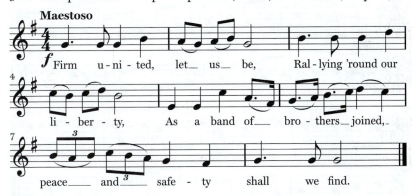

9.45 Philip Pile and Joseph Hopkinson, "Hail, Columbia" (adapted)

Maestoso

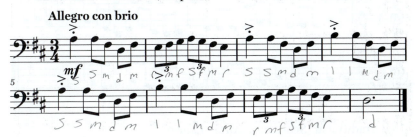

Firm   u - ni - ted,   let__ us__ be,   Ral - lying 'round our

li - ber - ty,   As   a   band of__   bro - thers__ joined,__

peace__ and   safe - ty   shall   we find.

9.46 Antonín Dvořák, Symphony No. 4, Op. 95, mvt. 4 (adapted)

Allegro con fuoco

9.47 Traditional (Ireland), "The Coolun"

9.48 Edvard Grieg, "Spring Dance," No. 1 from *Six Norwegian Mountain Melodies* (adapted)

9.49 Traditional (Scotland), "Annie Laurie"

9.50 Edvard Grieg, "Ranveig," Op. 66, No. 12

In m. 8, sing "*fi*" (♯4̂) for D♯.

♩ **Triplets**

A quarter-note triplet equals the duration of a half note.

Improvisation 9.4: Performing ♩ Triplets

1. Conduct or tap in two while performing patterns 1–9.

2. *Point and Sing:* Point to a rhythm pattern and perform it. Keeping a steady beat, point to a new pattern and perform it. Continue until you can perform all nine patterns accurately. Improvise eight-measure segments.

3. *Quick Composition:* Notate your favorite improvisation. Exchange with a peer. Conduct in two and perform your peer's rhythm aloud.

Rhythms

9.51

9.52

9.53

9.54

Harmonizing and Adding Counterpoint to a Melody

Keyboard and Improvisation 9.5: Harmonizing and Adding Counterpointing to a Melody

A. Harmonizing a Melody with Thirds and Sixths (Imperfect Consonances)

1. Play and sing this melody.

2. Play the melody and sing thirds below it. Switch parts and perform again.

3. Play the melody and sing sixths below it. Then sing the melody and play sixths below it.

6 6 6   6 6 6   6 6 6   6

B. Adding Counterpoint to a Melody

Good counterpoint features a mix of thirds and sixths and, occasionally, a PU, P5, or P8. Imperfect consonances may be consecutive, but perfect consonances may not.

While playing the melody from A.1, sing a counterpoint beneath it. Repeat this several times, trying different solutions each time.

U   3 3   6 6 3   3 6 5   6

C.

Follow the steps in A and B to harmonize and then add counterpoint to the following melody.

Duets

9.55 Traditional (United States), "Who Stole My Chickens"

9.56 Daniel Gottlob Türk, "The Hunters" (adapted)

CHAPTER 10

Plainchant, Melodic Embellishments, and Borrowed Beat Divisions in Compound Meter

In this chapter you'll learn to:

- Sing plainchant melodies
- Improvise embellishments in two-part counterpoint
- Perform two-part second-species contrapuntal exercises with a partner
- Perform borrowed beat divisions in compound meter (duplets and quadruplets)

Plainchant

Medieval sacred music featured modal melodies variously called plainchant, plainsong, or chant. Transcriptions replace the beautiful original notation with more-familiar symbols.

Melodies

Sing these plainchant transcriptions expressively using strategies from *Keyboard and Improvisation 9.1*. Rhythm values indicate "short" or "long" more than precise durations.

10.1 Plainchant, "*Veni Creator Spiritus*"

Melisma (>1 pitch per syllable)   Syllable emphasized   Breath

Ve – ni Cre – á - tor___ Spí - ri – tus,

Mén - tes   tu - ó – rum___   ví – si – ta:

Im – ple___   su –   pér – na___   grá - ti - a

Quae___   tu cre – á - sti___   péct – o - ra.

10.2 Plainchant, "*Pange lingua*"

Pan-ge lin-gua__ glo-ri - ó – si Cór – po-ris my-sté-ri-um,___

San-gui - nis-que pre - ti - ó - si, Quam in mun di pré ti um

Fru-ctus ven-tris ge - ne - ró - si Rex ef - fú-dit__ gén - ti-um.

10.3 Hildegard von Bingen, "*Caritas abundat in omnia*"

Ka   -   -   -   ri   -   -   -   tas__

___   a - bun - dat___

in___   om – ni   -   a

10.4 Plainchant, "*Salve Regina*"

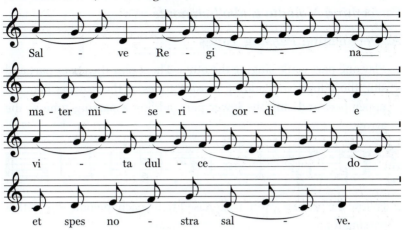

10.5 Plainchant, Antiphon for Vespers, from *Liber Usualis*

Melodic Embellishments in Two-Part Music

- A consonant-interval melodic skip is called a **consonant skip** (**CS**).
- **Passing tones** (**P**) fill the space between consonant skips with steps.
- **Suspensions** (**S**) are rhythmic displacements of consonant intervals.
- **Neighbor tones** (**N**) are the step above or below a prolonged melodic pitch.

Keyboard and Improvisation 10.1:
Performing Melodic Embellishments

A. Performing Passing Tones

1. Play one part while singing the other. Then, play the lower part and sing the upper part, adding passing tones at the arrows. Play the upper part and sing the lower part, adding a passing tone at the arrow.

2. Follow the process given in exercise 1 to fill each melodic skip with a passing tone.

(a)

(b)

(c)

B. Performing Suspensions

1. 7–6 suspensions

   Play one part while singing the other.

   In m. 2, sustain the upper pitches to create 7–6 suspensions.

2. 4–3 and 2–3 suspensions

Play one part while singing the other.

1   3   3   3   3   3   3   3   1

In m. 2, sustain the upper pitches to create 4–3 suspensions.

1   3   3   3   3   4–3 4–3 4–3   1

In m. 2, sustain the lower pitches to create 2–3 (bass) suspensions.

1   3   3   3   3   2–3 2–3 2–3   1

3. Use the steps in exercises 1 and 2 to add suspensions to each of the following exercises.

(a)

(b)

(c)

(d)

4. Play one part while singing the other. Then, write interval numbers between the staves.

5. Play the lower part as written and use the steps in exercises A and B to improvise an embellished version of the higher part. Then, play the higher part as written and improvise an embellished version of the lower part.

6. *Quick Composition:* Notate your favorite improvisation and perform it. Ask your peers to notate both melodic lines. Use exercises A and B as a basis for analyzing the counterpoint.

Example

Duets and Ensembles

Melodies 9.1–9.5 are now embellished with 2:1 counterpoint.

10.6 Johann Joseph Fux

10.7

10.8 Thomas Morley

10.9 Johann Joseph Fux

10.10

10.11 Anatoly Layadov

10.12

10.13 Johann Joseph Fux

10.14 Gioseffo Zarlino, from *The Art of Counterpoint* (adapted)

10.15 Gioseffo Zarlino, from *The Art of Counterpoint* (adapted)

10.16 William Byrd, Galliard to the Sixth Pavan, from
My Lady Nevell's Book

10.17 Orlando di Lasso, *Oculus non vidit*

O - cu - lus non vi - dit
O - cu - lus non
nec - au - ris au -
vi - dit nec - au -
- di - - - - vit,
- ris au - di - vit,

10.18 Thomas Weelkes, "Lady, Your Eye My Love Enforced"

10.19 John Dowland, "Now, O Now I Needs Must Part"

Now, O now I needs must part, Part - ing though I
Now, O now I needs must part, Part - ing though I
Now, O now I needs must____ part, Part - ing though I
Now, O now I needs must part, Part - ing though I

ab - sent mourn, Ab - sence can no joy im - part,
ab - sent mourn, Ab - sence can no joy im - part,
ab - sent mourn, Ab - sence can no joy im - part,
ab - sent mourn, Ab - sence can no joy im - part,

Joy once fled can - not re - turn.
Joy once fled can - not re - turn.
Joy once fled can - not re - turn.
Joy once fled can - not re - turn.

10.20 Orlando di Lasso, *Expectatio justorum laetitia*

Borrowed Beat Divisions in Compound Meters (Duplets and Quadruplets)

Improvisation 10.2: Performing Duplets and Quadruplets with a ♩. Beat Unit

Conduct or tap in two while performing patterns 1–9. Then, choose patterns randomly and improvise four-measure rhythms for a peer. While listening, the peer should write each pattern number. Then, have the peer perform your improvisation.

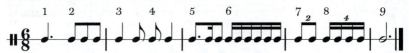

Rhythms

Duets

Improvisation 10.3: Performing Duplets and Quadruplets with a ♩. Beat Unit

Conduct or tap in two while performing patterns 1–9. Then, choose patterns randomly and improvise four-measure rhythms for a peer. While listening, the peer should write each pattern number. Then, have the peer perform your improvisation.

Rhythms

10.34

10.35

10.36

10.37

10.38

Duets

10.39

10.40

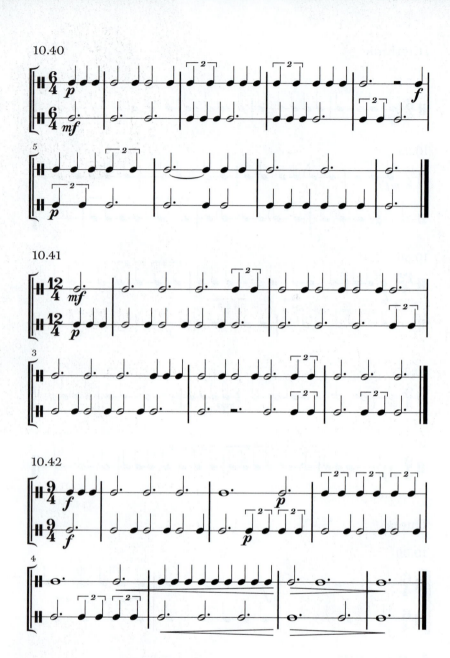

10.41

10.42

PART II

Diatonic Harmony
and Tonicization

CHAPTER 11

Eighteenth-Century Counterpoint and Eighth- and Dotted-Eighth-Note Beat Units

In this chapter you'll learn to:

- Perform two-part soprano-bass duets in eighteenth-century style
- Perform rhythms and melodies in simple and compound meter with eighth-note and dotted-eighth-note beat units
- Convert keyboard style to chorale style, also known as SATB

Soprano and Bass Lines in Eighteenth-Century Style

Compared with earlier music, eighteenth-century counterpoint features smaller beat-unit values, repeated notes that create more oblique motion, and sevenths that are treated as if they were chord tones. Though soprano and bass lines remain melodic, when the bass fulfills a harmonic role, these parts are no longer invertible.

Duets

Compare William Byrd's sixteenth-century Galliard with the eighteenth-century duets by Johann Sebastian Bach. Are Bach's lines invertible? How often does he use oblique motion and in what manner does he treat harmonic sevenths?

11.1 William Byrd, Galliard to the Sixth Pavan,
from *My Lady Nevell's Book*

11.2 Johann Sebastian Bach, *"O Ewigkeit, du Donnerwort"*
("O Eternity, Word of Thunder"), BWV 60

In measure 4, C♯ is *si* (♯$\hat{5}$).

11.3 Johann Sebastian Bach, *"Was Gott tut, das ist wohlgetan"* ("What
God Does Is Well Done"), BWV 99

11.4 Johann Sebastian Bach, *"Jesu, der du meine Seele"* ("Jesus, Who Saved My Soul"), BWV 78

11.5 Johann Sebastian Bach, *"Nun komm, der Heiden Heiland"* ("Now Come, Savior of the Gentiles"), BWV 61

In measure 5, hear *ti* ($\hat{7}$, A♯) in relation to *do* ($\hat{1}$).

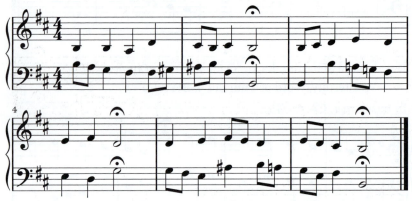

11.6 Johann Sebastian Bach, *"Wer nur den lieben Gott lässt walten"* ("He Lets Only Beloved God Rule"), BWV 93

In measure 3, tune *te* (♭$\hat{7}$) by imagining *do* ($\hat{1}1$) during the quarter rest.

11.7 Johann Sebastian Bach, *"Erhalt uns, Herr, bei deinem Wort"* ("Preserve Us, God, by Your Word"), BWV 126

11.8 Johann Sebastian Bach, *"Ich freue mich in dir"*
("I Rejoice in You"), BWV 133

Subdivided ♪ Beat Units

Improvisation 11.1: Performing ♪ Beat-Unit Rhythms

1. Point to a pattern and perform it. While keeping a steady beat, point
   to and perform a new pattern. Continue until you can perform all
   patterns accurately.

2. Ties, dots, and syncopation: Perform (a)-(c) to transform patterns
   4, 5, and 3 into new patterns 6, 7, and 8.

   (a) #4   + tie = #6   (b) #5   + tie = #7   (c) #3   + tie = #8

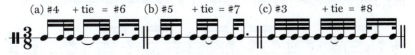

3. *Quick Composition:* Create rhythm compositions using these eight
   patterns. Exchange with a peer and perform each other's work.

Rhythms

Conduct meters $\frac{2}{8}$, $\frac{3}{8}$, and $\frac{4}{8}$ in two, three, or four, respectively. Beamed notes fall within a single beat. For comparison, exercises 11.9a–b are notated in different meters, but sound the same.

11.9a

Andante

11.9b

Andante

11.10

11.11

Moderato

11.12

Allegro

Presto

11.14

Moderately

11.15

Andante

11.16

Allegretto

Duets

11.17

Allegro

11.18

Subdivided ♪. Beat Units

Improvisation 11.2: Performing ♪. Beat-Unit Rhythms

Choose from patterns 1–5 and improvise a piece that is sixteen patterns long. Keep a steady tempo as you perform.

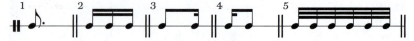

Rhythms

Exercises 11.20a and 11.20b sound the same, as do 11.21a and 11.21b.

11.20a

11.20b

11.21a

11.21b

11.22

11.23

11.24

Andantino

11.25

Allegro

Rhythmic Duets

11.26

Allegretto

11.27

11.28

Melodies

Depending on the meter signature, conduct in two, three, or four.

11.29 Béla Bartók, No. 16, from *44 Duets*, Vol. I (adapted)

Canon in two parts

11.30 Béla Bartók, No. 9, from *44 Duets*, Vol. I (adapted)

11.33 Kurt Weill and Maxwell Anderson, "September Song" (adapted)

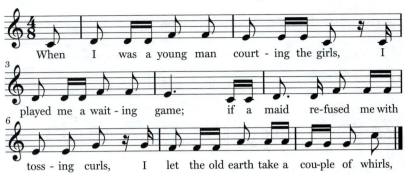

When I was a young man court - ing the girls, I

played me a wait - ing game; if a maid re-fused me with

toss - ing curls, I let the old earth take a cou-ple of whirls,

11.34 Traditional (American spiritual), "Just Now"

Andante

mp

11.35 Cécile Chaminade, *"L'amour captive"* ("Love, a Captive")

Allegretto

p

3

11.36 Herman Sandby, "Roselil"

mf-p

mp

mf

11.37

Brooding

11.38 Traditional (Ireland), "The Slashers"

Cheerfully

11.39 Traditional (Ireland), "A Veteran"

Andante

11.40 Philipp Friedrich Silcher, *"Die Soldatenbraut"* ("The Soldier's Bride") (adapted)

Moderately

11.41 Carolina Nairne, "The Laird O' Cockpen" (adapted)

11.42 Traditional (Germany), *"Untreue"* (Infidelity)

11.43 Traditional (Ireland), "Sorry the Day I Was Married"

11.44 Traditional (England), "At Winchester Was a Wedding" (adapted)

Melodic Duet

11.45 Muzio Clementi, Sonatina in C Major, Op. 36, No. 1, mvt. 3
Play one part and sing the other, or perform as a duet.

Keyboard Style

In keyboard style, the top three voices are played by the right hand while the bass voice is played by the left hand. The bass part is therefore more distinct from the other voices, and spacing is more flexible.

	Treble clef/right hand	*Bass clef/left hand*
Keyboard style	3 parts	1 part
SATB (Chorale style)	2 parts	2 parts

Keyboard 11.3: Converting Keyboard Style to SATB

1. Given music in keyboard style, there are two methods you might use to convert to SATB style. Method 1 produces more even voicing and makes it easier to keep voices within range; method 2 preserves the voicing of the keyboard-style version. Observing the given voice ranges, play each method of converting keyboard style to SATB.

Soprano	Alto	Tenor	Bass
C4–G5	G3–E5	C3–G4	E2–C4

Method 1	Method 2
Drop the alto one octave.	If the tenor is in range, notate it in bass clef.

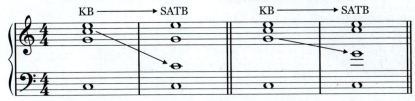

2. Play the specified triad in keyboard style. Then, convert it to SATB using method 1 or 2. Observe the voice ranges given in exercise 1.

Example: C major triad

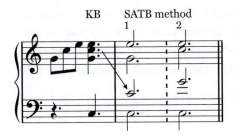

CHAPTER 12

Phrases, Cadences, and Subdivided Half- and Dotted-Half-Note Beat Units

In this chapter you'll learn to:

- Improvise phrases in pairs
- Perform music with half-note and dotted-half-note beat units
- Perform and recognize melodic T–D–T progressions

The Basic Phrase

Phrases are discrete musical thoughts that conclude with a cadence. *Inconclusive cadences* imply the music must continue, just as the comma in this sentence implies there's more to come. *Conclusive cadences* have a sense of finality, like that implied by the period at this end of this sentence.

Keyboard and Improvisation 12.1:
Performing Melodies in Phrase Pairs

1. While playing this keyboard progression, sing part 1 (the top line) in a comfortable range.

2. Play the progression again, but embellish part 1 with neighbor tones (N), chordal skips (CS), and/or passing tones (P). One possible improvisation is given.

3. Play the progression again, but sing part 2. Play again, but this time, embellish part 2.

4. Play the progression again, but sing part 3. Play again, but this time, embellish part 3.

5. Duet: Work with a partner. One person plays as the other sings. Switch roles and perform again.

Authentic and Half Cadences

The two most common cadence types are half and authentic. Study the chart to see their attributes.

Cadence type	Abbreviation	Melodic ending	Conclusive or inconclusive
Half	HC	re (2̂), ti (7̂), or sol (5̂)	inconclusive
Imperfect Authentic	IAC	mi (3̂) or sol (5̂)	inconclusive
Perfect Authentic	PAC	do (1̂)	conclusive

Melodies

As you perform, listen carefully to phrase endings and identify cadences as HC, IAC, or PAC.

12.1 James Lord Pierpont, "Jingle Bells"

For certain instrumental melodies such as the one that follows, it is often helpful to change octaves when the notes exceed your range. Here, for example, the last four notes can be sung an octave lower if they can't be sung where notated.

12.2 Gustav Mahler, Symphony No. 1, mvt. 1

12.3 Traditional (Germany), *"Ach, Du Lieber Augustin"*
("Oh, You Dear Augustin")

12.4 Giovanni Martini, Gavotte in F

12.5 Johann Sebastian Bach, Violin Concerto No. 1 in A Minor, mvt. 1

12.6 Johnny Marks, "Silver and Gold" (adapted)

Sil - ver and gold,   sil - ver and gold,

ev' - ry-one wish - es   for   sil - ver and   gold.

12.7 Thomas Bayly, "Long, Long Ago"

12.8 Gustav Mahler, Symphony No. 2, mvt. 2

12.9 Hank Cochran, "Make the World Go Away"

Do you re-mem-ber when you loved me
be-fore the world took me a - stray? If you do, then for-
give me, and make the world go a - way.

12.10 Traditional (Russia), *"Dubinushka"* ("Hammer Song")

12.11 Franz Schubert, *"Das Wandern"* ("Wandering"),
from *Die schöne Müllerin*

12.12 Gustav Mahler, Symphony No. 1, mvt. 3

Perform as a solo, or with four people as a canon in four parts.

12.13 Johann Sebastian Bach, *Burlesca*, from Partita No. 3
in A Minor, BWV 827

Ensembles

Sing the melody and accompany yourself at the keyboard, or sing as a five-part ensemble. Listen to phrase endings to identify whether cadences are HC, IAC, or PAC.

12.14 J. Rosamond Johnson and James Weldon Johnson, "Lift Every Voice and Sing" (adapted)

12.15 Joseph Haydn, String Quartet in D Major, Op. 50, No. 6, mvt. 1

Sing the tonic pitch, then *re* (2̂), the starting pitch.

12.16 Joseph Haydn, String Quartet in G Minor, Op. 20, No. 3, mvt. 1 (adapted)

For C♯, sing *fi*.

Harmonic Progression Études

These études outline tonic-dominant-tonic (T–D–T) progressions. Sing the melodies in their parallel minor keys, too.

12.17

I–V7–I

12.18

I–V7–I

12.19

Stem-down pitches represent the implied bass line.

I–V6–I

12.20

I–V$_5^6$–I

Subdivided ♩ Beat Units

Improvisation 12.2: Performing ♩ Beat-Unit Rhythms

1. Conduct or tap in two while performing the $\frac{2}{4}$ patterns. Still in two, perform the ¢ patterns, which sound identical.

2. Work with a partner. Choose randomly from the ¢ patterns until you have improvised four measures. As you perform, ask your partner to notate each pattern. Then, ask your partner to perform your improvisation. Switch roles and repeat the exercise.

Rhythms

12.21

12.25

Duets

12.26

12.27

Subdivided ♩. Beat Units

Improvisation 12.3: Performing ♩. Beat-Unit Rhythms

1. Conduct or tap in two while performing the $\frac{6}{8}$ patterns. Still in two, perform the $\frac{6}{4}$ patterns, which sound identical.

2. Work with a partner. Choose randomly from the $\frac{6}{4}$ patterns until you have improvised four measures. As you perform, ask your partner to listen and notate each pattern. Then, ask your partner to perform your improvisation. Switch roles.

Rhythms

12.28

Slowly

12.29

Moderato

Duets

12.34

Andante ma non troppo

Melodies

Though eighth notes beamed in groups of four may occur in **C**, when the beat unit is a 𝅗𝅥, as in **¢**, eighth notes are almost always beamed in groups of four. First, perform 12.36–12.37 in **C**. Perform again and accelerate the tempo until the meter sounds duple. Then, perform the melodies in **¢**.

12.36 Traditional (United States), "Lil' Liza Jane"

12.37 Traditional (American spiritual), "I Want to Climb Up Jacob's Ladder"

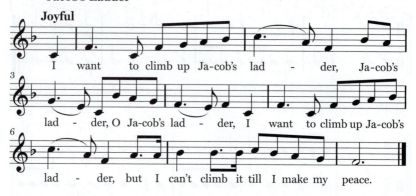

I want to climb up Ja-cob's lad - der, Ja-cob's lad - der, O Ja-cob's lad - der, I want to climb up Ja-cob's lad - der, but I can't climb it till I make my peace.

12.38 Traditional (France), *Dans notre village* ("In Our Village")

12.39 Traditional (United States), "The Good Old Way"

12.40 Traditional (England), "Rule, Britannia!"

12.41 Giovanni Gabrielli, *Canzon per sonar septimi toni a 8*

12.42 Johann Hermann Schein, Tripla from Suite No. 10 (adapted)

12.43 Traditional (Norway), *"Hjemland"* ("Homeland")

Slowly

mp

12.44 Traditional (England), "The Derby Ram"

Ben marcato

mf As I was go-ing to Der - by, all on a sun-shine day,_____ I met with the jol - li-est ram, Sir, that ev-er was fed on hay._____ In - deed, Sir, it's true, Sir, I ne'er was used to lie,_____ and if you had been at Der - by you'd have seen him as well as I!_____

Ensembles

12.45 François Couperin, "*Les moissonneurs*" ("The Reapers") (adapted)

12.46 Barbara Strozzi, "*Dessistete omai, pensieri*" ("Cease forever, thoughts"), from *Ariette a voce solo*, Op. 6

12.47 William Byrd, "The Carman's Whistle,"
from *My Lady Nevell's Book*

Part II Diatonic Harmony and Tonicization

CHAPTER 13

More Dominant Sevenths, Predominant Harmonies, and Syncopation

In this chapter you'll learn to:

- Perform and improvise music that includes inverted dominant seventh chords
- Perform and improvise music that includes predominant harmonies
- Perform syncopated rhythms

Resolving Dominant Seventh Chord Pitches

In melodic voice leading, dominant-seventh-chord pitches resolve as follows:

This V7-chord pitch...	usually resolves to this tonic-chord pitch...
ti (7̂)	do (1̂)
fa (4̂)	mi or me (3̂ or ♭3̂)
re (2̂)	do (1̂)
sol (5̂)	sol (5̂)

Memorize this melody to recall the resolutions. Sing in the parallel minor, too.

| ti | do | fa | mi | re | do | sol | sol |
| 7̂ | 1̂ | 4̂ | 3̂ | 2̂ | 1̂ | 5̂ | 5̂ |

Keyboard and Improvisation 13.1: Performing Inverted V7 Chords

1. Play the following phrase while singing part 1 in a comfortable range.

2. Play again, but this time, embellish part 1 with neighbor tones, chordal skips, and/or passing tones. One possible improvisation appears next.

3. Play the phrase, but sing part 2. Play again, while singing an embellishment of part 2.

4. *Duets:* Ask a partner to play while you sing an improvisation. Switch roles.

5. *Variations:* Perform again in parallel minor or in other keys.

Melodies

Melodies that imply dominant seventh chords include some or all of the pitches *sol-ti-re-fa* ($\hat{5}$-$\hat{7}$-$\hat{2}$-$\hat{4}$), especially the *fa-ti* ($\hat{4}$-$\hat{7}$) pair.

13.1 Franz Schubert, *Ecossaise* (adapted)

13.2 Leopold Mozart, Minuet (adapted)

13.3 Traditional (Hawai'i), *"Ua like no a like"* ("It Was All the Same")

13.4 Wolfgang Amadeus Mozart, Symphony No. 39, K. 543, mvt. 3, Trio (adapted)

13.5 Wolfgang Amadeus Mozart, Piano Sonata in G Major, K. 283, mvt. 3 (adapted)

13.6 Giuseppe Verdi, *"Questa o quella"* ("This or That"), from *Rigoletto*, Act 1, No. 2 (adapted)

13.7 Robert Schumann, *"Frühlingstraum"* ("Dream of Spring"),
from *Winterreise*

Sing *si* (#$\hat{5}$) for C#.

13.8 Robert Schumann, *"Silvesterlied"* ("New Year's Eve Song"), from
Album for the Young, Op. 68, No. 43 (adapted)

13.9 Anton Diabelli, Sonatina, Op. 168, mvt. 1 (adapted)

Ensemble

13.10 Joseph Haydn, String Quartet in G Major, Op. 3, No. 3, mvt. 1

Predominant Harmonies

Predominant-harmony bass pitch *fa* (4̂) usually rises to *sol* (5̂). In melodic voice leading, predominant-harmony pitches usually resolve as follows:

This predominant-harmony pitch...	*(often) falls toward this pitch...*
la or *le* (6̂ or ♭6̂)	*sol* (5̂)
fa (4̂)	*mi* or *me* (3̂ or ♭3̂)
re or *do* (2̂ or 1̂)	*ti* (7̂)

Keyboard and Improvisation 13.2:
Performing T-PD-D-T Phrases

1. Play each chord-number combination while singing part 1 in a comfortable range.

   (a) 1-2-3-4-5   (b) 1-4-5   (c) 5-6a-7   (d) 5-6b-7
   (e) 8-9-10-11   (f) 11-12a-13-14   (g) 11-12b-13-14

2. Play exercise 1 again, but this time, embellish part 1 with neighbor tones, chordal skips, and/or passing tones.

3. Play the entire piece, while singing part 1. Play again, and embellish part 1.

4. Play the entire piece, but sing part 2. Play again, but sing an embellishment of part 2.

5. Play the entire piece, but sing part 3. Play again, but sing an embellishment of part 3.

6. *Duets:* Ask a partner to play while you sing an improvisation. Switch roles.

7. *Variations:* Perform again in parallel minor or in other keys.

Melodies

These melodies include predominant harmonies.

13.11 Franz Schubert, *Zwanzig Walzer* (Twenty Waltzes), D. 146, No. 13 (adapted)

13.12 Robert Schumann, *"Frölicher Landmann"* ("The Happy Farmer"), from *Album for the Young*, Op. 68, No. 10 (adapted)

13.13 Béla Bartók, *For Children*, No. 1

Allegro

13.14 Georg Philipp Telemann, *Gigue à l'angloise*, TWV 32.2 (adapted)

13.15 Traditional (United States), "The Banks of Sacramento"

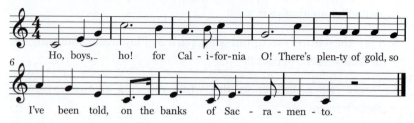

Ho, boys,_ ho! for Cal - i-for-nia O! There's plen-ty of gold, so

I've been told, on the banks of Sac - ra - men - to.

13.16 Johannes Brahms, Waltz, Op. 39, No. 3 (adapted)

13.17 Friedrich Burgmüller, *L'Arabesque*, Op. 100, No. 2 (adapted)

Allegro scherzando

13.18 Traditional (United States), "The Lane County Bachelor"

My_ name is Frank Bale an old bach-'lor I am,_ I'm

keep-in' old batch on an el - e-gant plan._ You'll find me out West in the

coun-ty of Lane, Starv-ing to death on a gov-ern-ment claim.

Ensembles

13.19 Joseph Haydn, String Quartet in F Major, Op. 3, No. 5, mvt. 2 (adapted)

13.20 Johann Christian Bach, Sonata in C Minor, Op. 17, No. 2, mvt. 3

Syncopated Beats and Beat Divisions

Syncopation accentuates a beat or a part of the beat that is normally weak.

Rhythms

These rhythms feature syncopations that accent a metrically weak beat.

13.21

13.22

13.23

13.24

13.25

13.26

The next rhythms feature syncopations that accent a metrically weak beat *division*.

13.27

13.28

13.29

13.30

13.31

Part II Diatonic Harmony and Tonicization

13.32

13.33

13.34

Rhythmic Duets

13.35

13.36

13.37

Allegro

13.38

Moderately

13.39

Con moto

Melodies

13.40 Al Kasha and Joel Hirschborn, "Candle on the Water"

I'll be your can-dle on the wa - ter,

My love for you will al-ways burn.   I know you're

lost   and drift-ing,   but the clouds are lift - ing,

don't give up, you have some-where to   turn.

13.41 Franz Liszt, *Hungarian Rhapsody* No. 14

13.42 M. Kealoha, *"Malana'i Anu Ka Makani"* ("The Wind Was Cold")

13.43 George Halket, *"Logie, o' Buchan"*

13.44 Redd Stewart and Pee Wee King, "Tennessee Waltz"

I was waltz-ing_ with my dar-lin'_ to the Ten-nes - see_

Waltz_ when an old friend I hap-pened to_ see._

13.45 Traditional (United States), "The Inquisitive Lover"

13.46 Traditional (Hungary), *"Magasan Repül A Daru"*
("Hungary's Treasure")

13.47 Traditional (Italy), *"La vera sorrentina"* ("The True Sorrentine Woman") (adapted)

13.48 Léo Delibes, *Le jardin animé* (The Animated Garden) (adapted)

Melodic Duet

13.49 Béla Bartók, "Smooth Syncopations," No. 19 from *First Term at the Piano*

$\frac{6}{4}$ Chords, Melody Harmonization, and Swing Rhythm

In this chapter you'll learn to:

- Sing and recognize $\frac{6}{4}$ chords and predominant chords
- Perform music with swing rhythms
- Harmonize melodies

$\frac{6}{4}$ Chords

Historically, six-four ($\frac{6}{4}$) chords only appear in these four ways:

$\frac{6}{4}$ type	How to recognize it
Arpeggiated	Triad's fifth is the lowest pitch
Passing	Harmonizes the passing tone in a voice exchange
Neighboring (Pedal)	Prolongs a triad's 3rd and 5th with their upper neighbors
Cadential	Delays the resolution to the 3rd and 5th of the V chord: e.g., *mi→re* ($\hat{3}$→$\hat{2}$) and *do→ti* ($\hat{1}$→$\hat{7}$)

Melodies

These études highlight the four types of $\frac{6}{4}$ chords. Stem-down pitches imply the bass line.

Arpeggiated $\frac{6}{4}$

14.1

Same triad arpeggiated

Bb   I   I⁶   I⁶₄   I

14.2

Passing $\frac{6}{4}$

14.3

14.4

Neighboring (Pedal) $\frac{6}{4}$ Bass stays the same

14.5

14.6

Cadential $^6_4$

14.7

14.8

Keyboard and Improvisation 14.1: Performing $^6_4$ Chords

1. Play the following phrase while singing part 1 in a comfortable range.

2. Play again, but this time, embellish part 1 with chordal skips, passing tones, and/or neighbor tones. One possible improvisation is provided here.

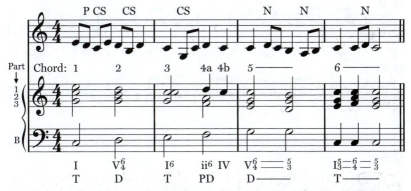

3. Play the phrase, but sing part 2. Play again, while singing an embellishment of part 2.

4. Play the phrase, but sing part 3. Play again, while singing an embellishment of part 3.

5. *Duets:* Ask a partner to play while you sing an improvisation. Switch roles.

6. *Variations:* Perform again in parallel minor or in other keys.

Swing Rhythm

In swing rhythm, simple-meter beat divisions are performed unequally (long-short) similar to compound-meter beat divisions. The shorter, offbeat notes are stressed and the music is generally syncopated. Compare the first two rhythms, 14.9 and 14.10: To perform the straight eighth notes in the $\frac{2}{4}$ example with swung rhythms, sing the equivalent measures in the $\frac{6}{8}$ example.

Rhythms

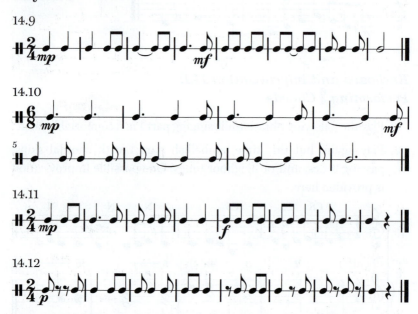

14.9

14.10

14.11

14.12

Mid-twentieth-century music sometimes indicates swing using dotted notes.

14.13

Moderate swing

14.14

Andante

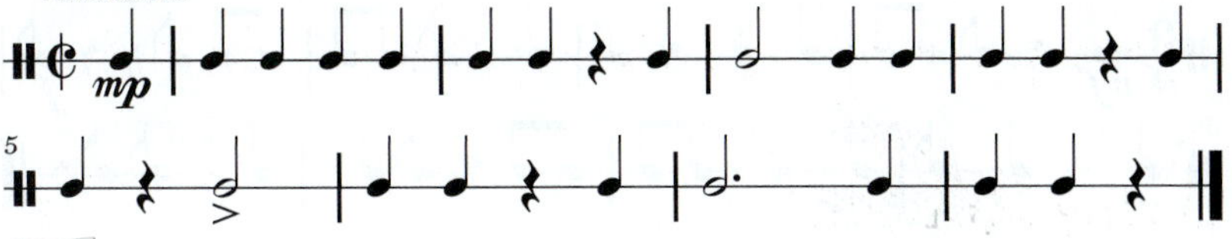

14.15

Fast

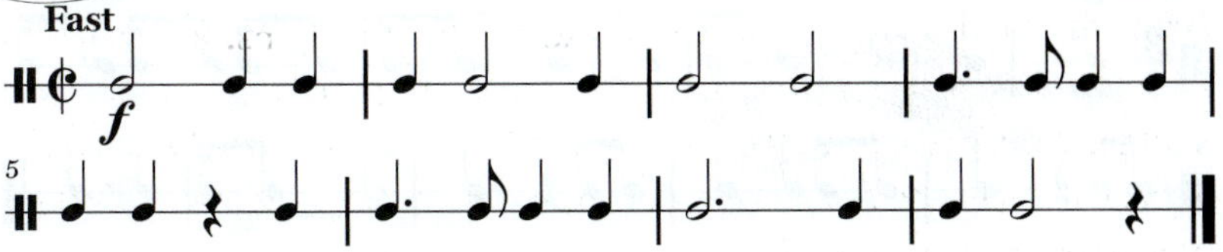

14.16

Andante

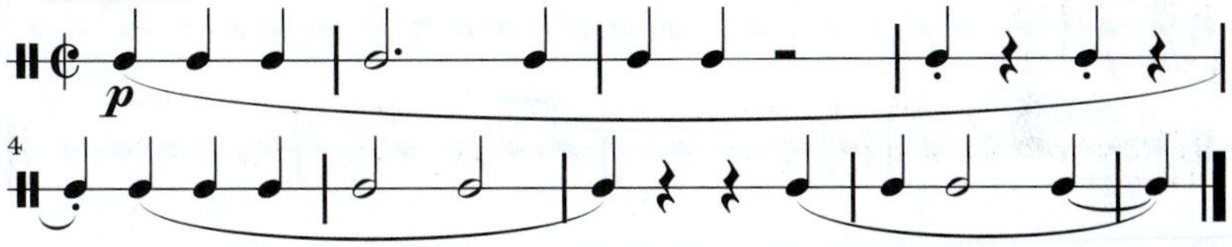

14.17

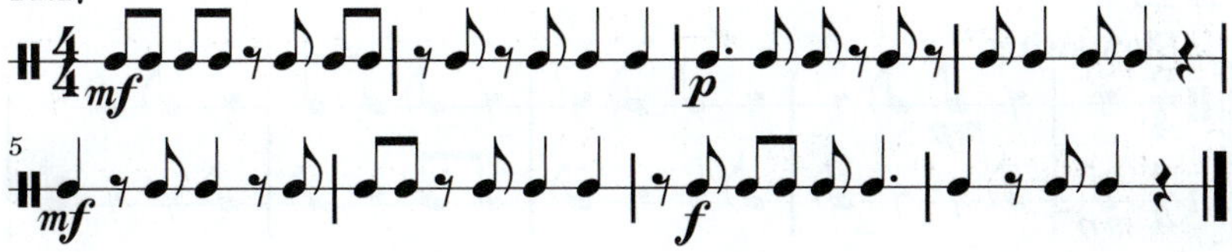

14.18

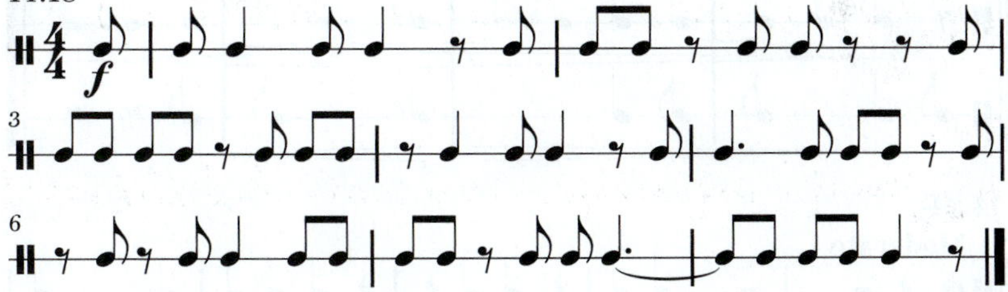

14.19

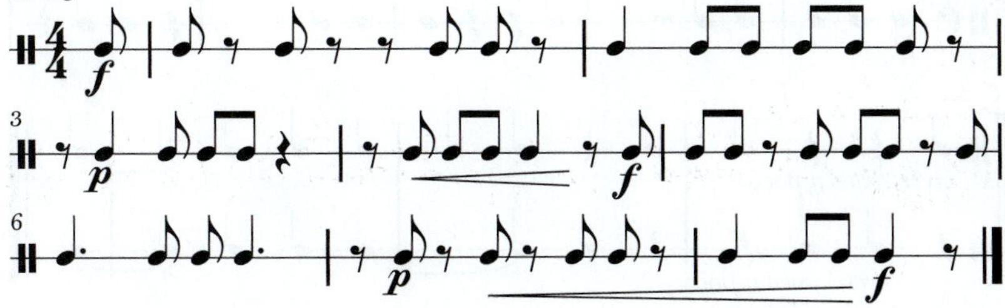

14.20

Bright swing

14.21

Allegretto

14.22

Moderate swing

Duets

14.23

Slow swing

14.24

Moderato

14.28

Melodies

Perform these melodies with swing rhythms.

14.29

Moderately

14.30

Lively

14.31

Up tempo

14.32

Misterioso

 14.33

Emphatically

14.34 Horace Silver, "The Preacher"

He would stand up there in the pul - pit,

horn in his hand,___ and let that

mel - o - dy take___ you to the Prom - ised Land.___

14.35 Frank Perkins, "Stars Fell on Alabama"

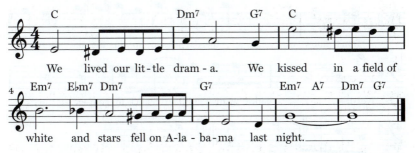

We lived our lit - tle dram - a. We kissed in a field of

white and stars fell on A - la - ba - ma last night.___

14.36 Traditional (United States), "The Crawdad Song"

14.37 Jule Styne and Sammy Cahn, "It's Been a Long, Long Time"

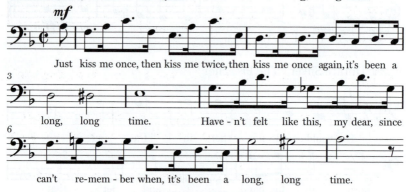

Just kiss me once, then kiss me twice, then kiss me once again, it's been a long, long time. Have-n't felt like this, my dear, since can't re-mem-ber when, it's been a long, long time.

The two-beat feel of slow jazz is often notated in cut time, but can be imagined as common time with a quarter-note beat around 60.

14.38 Ted Koehle and Harold Arlen, "Stormy Weather"

Don't know why_____ there's no sun up in the sky, Storm-y Weath-er,_____ Since my man and I_____ ain't to-geth-er,_____ keeps rain-in' all____ the time._____

Melody Harmonization

Melodic pitches imply harmonies. When melodies emphasize or prolong *do*, *mi*, or *sol* ($\hat{1}$-$\hat{3}$-$\hat{5}$), they imply tonic, I. Melodies emphasizing *sol*, *ti*, *re*, or *fa* ($\hat{5}$-$\hat{7}$-$\hat{2}$-$\hat{4}$) imply dominant, V$^{(7)}$.

Keyboard and Improvisation 14.2: Harmonizing Melodies

1. Play this progression three times, while singing parts 1, 2, and 3, respectively.

2. Transpose the progression to G, D, and F major, playing while singing in each key.

3. Harmonize melodies 14.39-14.43 using the chords in exercise 1. Play chord 1 and begin singing the melody. Change chords using the rhythm above the melody.

   • Chords 1-2 work well during phrases or to create a half cadence.

   • Chords 3-5 create a perfect authentic cadence.

14.39 Ludwig van Beethoven, Symphony No. 9, mvt. 4 (adapted)

14.40 Wolfgang Amadeus Mozart, Serenade in G,
Eine kleine Nachtmusik, K. 525, mvt. 1

14.41 Franz Schubert, *"Wiegenlied"* ("Lullaby") (adapted)

14.42 Joseph Haydn, Symphony No. 13, mvt. 1

14.43 George Frideric Handel, Hornpipe, from *Water Music*, Suite No. 2, HWV 349 (adapted)

CHAPTER 15

Root Progressions, Syncopated Subdivisions, More Cadences, and Modal Melodies

In this chapter you'll learn to:

- Sing and recognize diatonic root progressions in melodic contexts
- Perform syncopated beat subdivisions
- Harmonize melodies using Phrygian, plagal, and deceptive resolutions
- Sing more-challenging modal melodies

Diatonic Root Progressions

Common-practice music often features these three root movements:

Root movement	Common examples
Descending fifth *Ascending fourth*	I–IV; V–I; vi–ii
Descending third *Ascending third*	I–vi; vi–IV; IV–ii
Ascending second	I–ii; IV–V; V–vi

Keyboard and Improvisation 15.1: Performing Diatonic Root Progressions

1. Identify each of the three types of diatonic root progression in the following example. Then, play it while singing the soprano with syllables or numbers.

B♭:   I   vi   IV   V   I   ii⁶   V7   I

2. Play again, this time embellishing the soprano with neighboring tones, chordal skips, and passing tones.

3. *Duet:* Play the example and ask a partner to improvise an embellished melody. Switch roles.

4. *Quick Composition:* Notate the melody of your favorite improvisation. Exchange melodies with a peer and sing each other's work with syllables or numbers.

Melodies

Identify root progressions in these études by type: fifth, third, or second. Stem-down pitches imply the bass line.

15.1

15.6

Syncopated Beat Subdivisions

Stressing a normally unaccented beat subdivision creates syncopation. Such syncopated notes can be described as either *moving toward* or *moving from* a stronger beat.

Rhythms

15.7

Andante

15.8

Slowly

15.9

Andante

15.10

Allegretto

15.11

Allegro

15.12

Andante

15.13

Steadily

15.14

Andante

15.15

Grazioso

15.16

Moderato

Duets

15.17

Andante

15.18

Tempo guisto

15.19

15.20

15.21

Melodies

15.22 Traditional (American emancipation song),
"Many Thousand Gone"

15.23 Traditional (England), "Rigs o' Marlow"

15.24 Traditional (Great Britain), "Lord Thomas and Fair Ellendor"

15.25 Traditional (American emancipation song), "By an' By" (adapted)

15.26 J. Denver, B. Danoff, and T. Nivert, "Take Me Home, Country Roads"

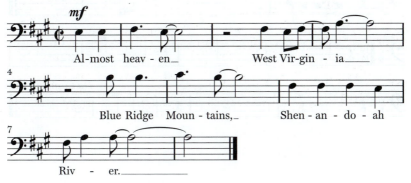

Al-most heav - en_ West Vir-gin - ia_

Blue Ridge Moun - tains,_ Shen - an - do - ah

Riv - er._

15.27 Traditional (England), "Laudanum Bunches"

15.28 Traditional (United States), "Come All You Fair
   and Tender Ladies"

15.29 Traditional (American spiritual), "Can't You Live Humble?"
   (adapted)

15.30 Elton John and Tim Rice, "Can You Feel the Love Tonight?"

And can you feel_ the love_____ to-night,____
how it's laid_ to rest?__ It's e-nough__ to make
kings_ and_ vag-a-bonds_ be-lieve the ver - y best.____

15.31 Johann Sebastian Bach, Chorale Prelude *Wen nur den lieben Gottläßt walten*" ("Who Only Lets Dear God Rule")

New Cadence Types

Phrygian, plagal, and deceptive cadences and resolutions can be implied by melodies.

Keyboard and Improvisation 15.2: Performing Phrygian, Plagal, and Deceptive Resolutions

A. Phrygian Half Cadence: iv⁶–V

15.32 Traditional (United States), "On the Erie Canal"

1. Play keyboard measures 1-2 four times, singing each part with syllables or numbers.

2. Play keyboard measures 1-2 in a loop, this time improvising melodic embellishments on part 1, the keyboard soprano.

3. Sing the traditional melody (notated separately on the treble staff). Then, sing it again while accompanying yourself.

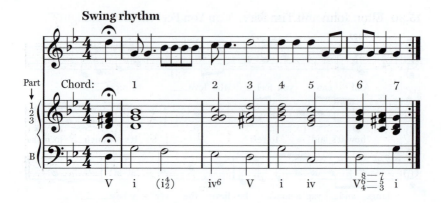

B. Plagal (iv–i) and Deceptive Resolutions (V–VI) with a Phrygian Cadence (ii$^4_3$–V)

15.33 Amy Beach, "Forgotten" (adapted)

1. Play the keyboard accompaniment four times, singing each keyboard part with syllables or numbers.

2. Sing the top treble-staff melody by itself. Then, sing it again while accompanying yourself.

C. Plagal Cadence: iv–i or IV–I

Following the steps in A and B; sing each keyboard part and then sing the melody while accompanying yourself at the keyboard.

15.34 Amy Beach, "Barcarolle"

15.35 Traditional (United States), "We Three Kings"

Modal Melodies

Sing these modal melodies using either parallel- or relative-solfège syllables as explained in *Keyboard and Improvisation 9.1.*

15.36 Béla Bartók, No. 37 from *44 Duets*, Vol. II (adapted)

15.37 Traditional (Great Britain), "Cumberland Nelly"

The melody concludes on its final, E.

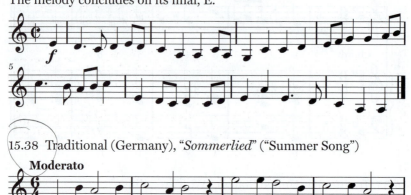

15.38 Traditional (Germany), "*Sommerlied*" ("Summer Song")

Moderato

15.39 Traditional, "Wondrous Love"

Peacefully

15.40 John Logan, "Consolation," from *Sixteen Tune Settings* (1812)

15.41 Béla Bartók, *Hungarian Folk Song*

15.42 Martin Luther, *"Aus tiefer Not schrei ich zu dir"*
("From Deep Distress I Cry to You") (adapted)

Andante

15.43 Béla Bartók, No. 18 from *44 Duets*, Vol. I (adapted)

15.44 Traditional (Great Britain), "The Bird Song"

Hi say the black - bird, sit - ting on a chair,

Once I court - ed a la - dy fair; She proved fick-le and

turned her back, and ev - er since then I've dressed in black.

15.45 Traditional (China), "Dance of Youth"

15.46 Traditional (Great Britain), "Bessie Bell and Mary Gray"

Duet

15.47 Béla Bartók, No. 39 from *44 Duets*, Vol. II (adapted)

CHAPTER 16

Melodic Embellishment, Harmonizing Modal Melodies, and Compound Triplets

In this chapter you'll learn to:

- Recognize, perform, and create melodies with melodic embellishments
- Harmonize modal melodies
- Perform rhythms that contain compound (super) triplets

Embellishing Tones

Sustaining the effect of a pitch or chord is called prolongation. Often, prolongation occurs by means of melodic embellishment.

	Embellishing tone	Symbol	What it is
Consonant	Consonant skip	CS	Skip or leap between chord tones
Dissonant	Suspension/ Retardation	S	Rhythmically delayed melodic resolution
	Neighbor tone	N	Note above or below the prolonged pitch
	Anticipation	A	Melodic resolution occurring earlier than expected
	Passing tone	P	Note filling the gap between between consonant-skip pitches

Keyboard and Improvisation 16.1: Embellishing Melodic Outlines

1. Play both parts while singing the upper part. Play again, but embellish the upper part with consonant skips (CS), passing

tones (P), and neighbor tones (N). Ask listeners to identify each improvised embellishment: CS, P, or N. Note: The implied chords are provided for you above the grand staff.

Traditional (United States), "Goodnight, Ladies"
(simplified melodic outline)

2. Variations:

   a. Perform in the parallel minor key and include the leading tone.

   b. Perform as a duet, one person per staff.

   c. Improvise an embellished melody while a peer sings the lower part.

3. *Quick Composition:* Notate your favorite improvisation. Include the correct key and meter signature. Exchange with a peer and sing and analyze each other's melody.

Melodies

Identify the embellishments in these melodies: consonant skips; diatonic or chromatic passing tones; and diatonic, chromatic, incomplete, or complete neighbor tones.

16.1 Irving Berlin, "White Christmas"

16.2 Bert Kaempfert, "Strangers in the Night"

16.3 Jerome Kern, "The Song Is You"

16.4 Felix Mendelssohn, *Song without Words*, Op. 62, No. 4 (adapted)

16.5 John Hill Hewitt, "All Quiet along the Potomac Tonight"

Tune *fi* (♯4̂) in measure 14 by hearing its resolution to *sol* (5̂) in measure 15 as part of a double neighbor figure.

bat - tle;_____ Not an of - fi - cer lost! On-ly one of the

men Moan-ing out all a - lone the death rat - tle._____

16.6 Gene Lees and Amando Manzanero, "Yesterday I Heard the Rain"

Slowly
mp

Yes - ter - day I heard the rain, whis-per - ing your name,

(echo)

ask-ing where you'd gone. It fell soft - ly from the clouds

(echo)

on the si - lent crowds as I wan-dered on.

16.7 Richard Rodgers and Lorenz Hart, "Bewitched"

Moderately
mp

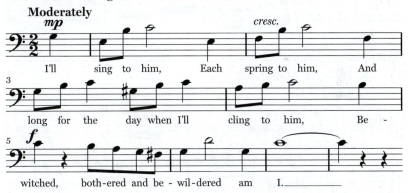

I'll sing to him, Each spring to him, And

long for the day when I'll cling to him, Be -

f

witched, both-ered and be - wil-dered am I._____

16.8 Ned Washington and Leigh Harline, "When You Wish Upon a Star"

Sweetly
mp

If your heart is in your dream, no re-quest is too ex-treme,

when you wish up - on a star as dream - ers do.

16.9 A. Lloyd Webber, C. Hart, and R. Stilgoe, "All I Ask of You" (adapted)

All I ask for is one love, one life-time; say the word and I will fol-low you.___ Share each day with me, each night, each morn-ing. Love me, that's all I ask of you.

To improve your proficiency with solfège or numbers, practice the following melodies slowly, then gradually increase the tempo.

16.10 Joseph Haydn, Piano Sonata No. 40 in G Major, mvt. 3 (adapted)

16.11 Wolfgang Amadeus Mozart, String Quartet No. 2 in D Major, K. 155, mvt. 1 (adapted)

16.12 Wolfgang Amadeus Mozart, Piano Sonata in D Major, K. 311, mvt. 3 (adapted)

Duets

16.13 Joseph Haydn, Piano Sonata No. 5 in C Major, Menuetto

16.14 Ludwig van Beethoven, Ecossaise in G (adapted)

16.15 Béla Bartók, No. 39, from *44 Duets*, Vol. II

Compound (Super) Triplets

In compound (super) triplets, three notes occur during the span of two beats.

Rhythms

Imagine the stems-down rhythm when performing the compound triplets.

16.16

Compare measures 3, 6, and 7 of 16.17a and 16.17b.

16.17a Compound (super) triplets, which are evenly spaced

16.17b Broadway or rumba "triplets," which are unequal (3 + 3 + 2)

16.18

16.19

16.20

16.21

16.22

16.23

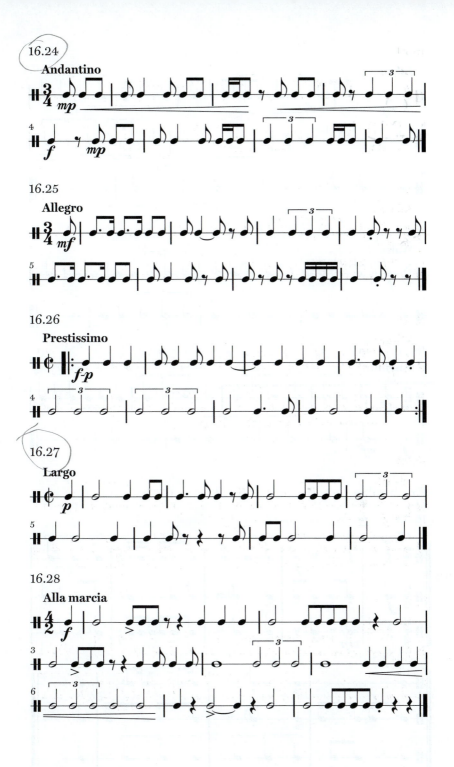

16.29

16.30

16.31

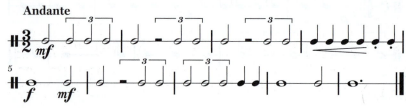

Ensembles

16.32

16.33

16.34

16.35

16.36

16.37

Harmonizing Aeolian, Dorian, and Mixolydian Melodies

Melodic pitches $\hat{1}$-$\hat{3}$-$\hat{5}$ imply tonic and $\hat{5}$-$\hat{7}$-$\hat{2}$ imply dominant. In Aeolian, Dorian, and Mixolydian, the dominant chord's quality is minor.

Keyboard and Improvisation 16.2: Performing Modes with Minor Dominants

1. Choose a mode and use its key signature to play the progression three times, singing parts 1, 2, and 3, respectively.

2. Play again in the mode of your choice, this time embellishing part 1 with consonant skips, passing tones, and neighboring tones.

Melodies

Harmonize melodies 16.37-16.43 using the modal T–D–T progressions given in *Keyboard and Improvisation 16.2*.

Chords 1–2 work well to begin or continue phrases, or to create a half cadence.

Chords 3–5 create a perfect authentic cadence.

16.38 Traditional (Canada), "Canoeing Song" (Aeolian)

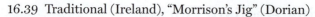

16.40 Traditional (England), "Scarborough Fair" (Dorian)

16.41 Traditional (Ireland), "Erin's Lovely Home" (Dorian)

one, Then___ I___ be - came a ser - vant ___ un - to some gen - tle man. I___ served him true___ and hon - est, and___ that is ver-y well known, But___ cru - el - ly he ban - ish'd me from E - rin's___ love - ly home.

16.42 Traditional (Appalachia, United States), "The Three Ravens" (Mixolydian)

16.43 George Gershwin and Ira Gershwin, "Oh, Lord, I'm on My Way," from *Porgy and Bess* (adapted) (Mixolydian)

16.44 Traditional (England), "The Rambling Sailor" (Mixolydian)

Delayed Resolutions

Suspensions and retardations embellish a harmony by delaying its resolution.

Keyboard and Improvisation 16.3: Performing Delayed Resolutions

1. Play chords 1, 2, and 4, singing part 1 or 2. Then, perform chords 1-4 to create each type of delayed resolution.

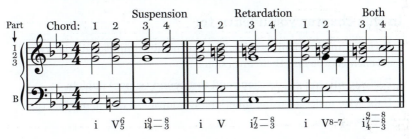

2. Work in pairs. One person plays the entire exercise while the other improvises embellishments of either part 1 or part 2.

CHAPTER 17

Diminished Chords, Mixed Beat Divisions, and Compound Duplets

In this chapter you'll learn to:

- Perform and harmonize melodies that include diminished triads and seventh chords and their inversions
- Perform mixed beat divisions and compound (super) duplets
- Improvise melodies using functionally equivalent dominant-function chords

Diminished Triads and Seventh Chords

Diminished triads and seventh chords contain *ti* (7̂) and *fa* (4̂), which resolve to *do* (1̂) and *mi* (3̂), respectively. In diminished seventh chords, the chordal seventh, whether *le* (♭6̂) or *la* (6̂), resolves down to *sol* (5̂).

Improvisation 17.1: Performing Diminished Triads and Seventh Chords

Choose a rhythm and a chord: vii°7, vii∅7, or vii°. Then, improvise a melody that outlines the chosen chord with the chosen rhythm. End on *do* (1̂).

Example: Choose rhythm 2 and vii∅7.

(1)
Moderato

(2)
Waltz

(3)
March

(4)
Sweetly

Melodies

17.1 Johann Sebastian Bach, Fugue in C Minor, BWV 546

Measure 3 outlines a vii°7.

17.2 Joseph Haydn, Piano Sonata in C Major, Hob. XVI:21,
   mvt. 1 (adapted)

17.3 Johann Sebastian Bach, Invention No. 4 in D Minor, BWV 775

Measure 2 outlines a vii°7, which has been filled in with passing tones.

17.4 Ludwig van Beethoven, String Quartet in F Major, Op. 18, No. 1, mvt. 2 (adapted)

The arrows show a vii°7, which is filled in with passing tones and embellished with a chromatic lower neighbor.

Duets

17.5 Joseph Haydn, Piano Sonata in D Major, Hob. XVI:24, mvt. 2 (adapted)

17.6 Johann Sebastian Bach, Double I from Violin Partita No. 1 in B Minor (adapted)

In measure 1, *ti* (7̂) and *le* (♭6̂) suggest vii°7. Follow the guide tones in the lower staff to help you perform this compound melody.

Mixed Beat Divisions

Compound beats may appear in simple meters and vice versa. Such "borrowed" beat divisions are called "tuplets." A tuplet's number indicates the number of parts into which a beat divides. A triplet, for example, divides a simple-meter beat into thirds.

Melodies

17.7 Franz Liszt, *Hungarian Rhapsody* No. 15

17.8 Gustav Mahler, Symphony No. 2, mvt. 5 (adapted)

17.9 Ernest Chausson, *"Les papillons,"* Op. 2, No. 3

17.10 Frédéric Chopin, Nocturne in G Minor, Op. 37, No. 1

17.11 Amy Beach, *"Chanson d'amour"* ("Song of Love")

17.12 Johann Sebastian Bach, Fugue in E Minor, from
The Well-Tempered Clavier, Book II, BWV 879

17.13 Traditional (United States), *"Aine, dé, trois, Caroline"*
("One, Two, Three, Caroline")

17.14 Traditional (Louisiana, United States) *"Belle Layotte"*

17.15 Johannes Brahms, *"Guter Rat"* ("Good Advice"), Op. 75, No. 2,
from *Four Ballades and Romances* (adapted)

17.16 Sebastián Iradier, *"La Paloma"* ("The Dove")

17.17 A. Lewis, V. Stock, and L. Rose, "Blueberry Hill"

The moon stood still_____ on Blue-ber-ry Hill_____

_ and lin-gered un - til_____ my dreams came true.____

Ensembles

17.18 Joseph Haydn, Piano Sonata No. 18 in B♭ Major, mvt. 2 (adapted)

17.19 Maciej Radziwill, *Polonaise* (adapted)

Tapping the eighth notes will help you perform the triplet correctly. Sing the melody while playing the bass, or perform as a trio.

17.20 Joseph Haydn, String Quartet in F Major, Op. 3, No. 5, mvt. 2, Trio (adapted)

This étude features the progressions i–vii°7–i, i–vii°6–i6, and i–vii°$_3^4$–i6.
Play the left-hand part while singing the right in a comfortable register.

17.21

Compound (Super) Duplets

Compound (super) duplets occur when two notes span three beats.

Rhythms

Imagine the stems-down notes while performing the compound duplets.

17.22

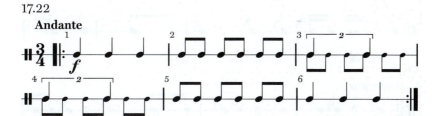

Rhythm 17.23 is non-retrogradable, meaning it sounds the same
forward and backward, like a musical palindrome.

17.23

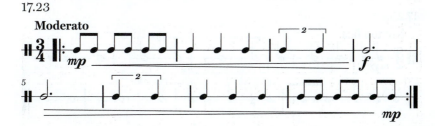

In rhythms 17.30–17.31, imagine the stems-down rhythm when performing the compound duplets.

17.30

17.31

17.32

17.33

17.34

17.40

17.41

Duets

17.42

17.43

17.44

17.45

17.46

17.47

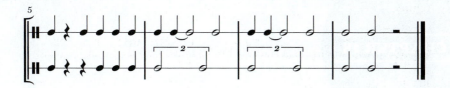

Functionally Equivalent Dominant-Function Chords

Leading-tone seventh chords are functionally equivalent to V7 and leading-tone triads are functionally equivalent to V. When one chord substitutes for the other, the voice leading remains the same.

Keyboard and Improvisation 17.2:
Performing Functionally Equivalent Dominant Chords

1. For V7 or V, perform chords 1–2a–3. For vii°7 or vii°6, perform chords 1–2b–3.

2. Choose a progression and a part. Play the progression while singing the part. Perform again, this time singing a melodic embellishment of the part. Choose a different part and repeat the process. Ask a partner to listen and identify the dominant-function chord and the melodic embellishments.

CHAPTER 18

Phrase Structure, Melody Harmonization, and Syncopation with Borrowed Beat Divisions

In this chapter you'll learn to:

- Sing and recognize a variety of phrase structures
- Improvise parallel and contrasting periods
- Harmonize melodies that include predominants
- Perform syncopations that incorporate borrowed beat divisions

Phrase Subdivisions, Sentence, and Independent Phrase

Phrases can contain smaller units called subphrases, which themselves may consist of or contain a motive.

Phrase:	the smallest complete idea that ends with a cadence
Subphrase:	a cohesive part of a phrase
Motive:	a recurring idea with distinct rhythm and contour
Sentence:	a phrase made from three subphrases with the proportion 1:1:2
Independent phrase:	an isolated phrase that ends with a PAC

Melodies

18.1 Franz Schubert, String Quartet in E♭ Major, Op. 125, No. 1, mvt. 2 (adapted)

18.2 Johann Sebastian Bach, Fugue in C Minor, from
   The Well-Tempered Clavier, Book I, BWV 847

18.3 Pauline Duchambge, "*Rondes des pauvres*" ("Round of the Poor")

18.4 George Frideric Handel, Sonatina, HWV 585 (adapted)

18.5 Ludwig van Beethoven, Piano Sonata in C Major, Op. 2, No. 1,
   mvt. 1 (adapted)

18.6 George Gershwin and Ira Gershwin, "'S Wonderful"

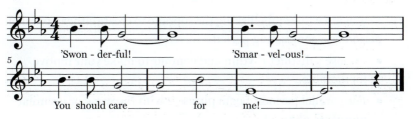

18.7 Nancy Gifford, "I'll Raise You!" from *Remember the Ladies*

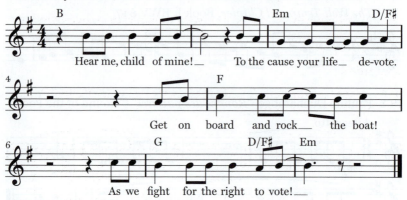

Periods

Phrases often group in antecedent-consequent pairs called periods. Same or similar melodic beginnings receive the same letter name. A contrasting beginning receives a new letter name. Phrase diagrams show structural levels, cadences, and unit names.

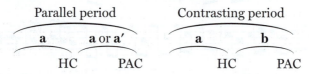

Keyboard and Improvisation 18.1: Performing Parallel and Contrasting Periods

1. Play the progression while singing the soprano in a comfortable register.

2. Play again while embellishing the soprano to create either a parallel period or a contrasting period.

   • Choose a distinct rhythm and contour to make your motive memorable.

   • For parallel periods, begin phrase 2 with the same or a similar motive as phrase 1.

- For contrasting periods, begin phrase 2 with a different motive.

3. Ask listeners to notate the motive of each phrase or to diagram the phrase structure.

Melodies

18.8 Based on Wolfgang Amadeus Mozart's Piano Sonata in D Major, K. 576, mvt. 1 (adapted)

18.9 Based on the traditional Shaker melody "Simple Gifts"

18.10 Based on Felix Mendelssohn's "Spring Song," from *Songs without Words*, Op. 62, No. 6 (adapted)

18.11 Robert Nathaniel Dett, "Listen to the Lambs" (adapted)

He shall feed his flock like a shep - herd, and car - ry the young lambs in— his bo - som.

18.12 Traditional (Puerto Rico), *El coquí* ("Little Frog")

18.13 Clara Schumann, *"Sie liebten dich beide"* ("They Once Loved Each Other"), Op. 13, No. 2

18.14 Lizzie Doirin, *"Mai Poina Oe Iau"* ("Do Not Forget Me")

18.15 Tony Velona and Remo Capra, *"O Bambino"*

18.16 Tom Blackburn and George Bruns, "Ballad of Davy Crockett"

Born on a moun-tain top in Ten - nes - see, Green-est state in the land of the free, Raised in the woods so's he knew ev-'ry tree, kilt him a b'ar when he was on - ly three.

Periods can comprise two or more sentences, and sometimes, three or more phrases.

18.17 Traditional (United States), "Clementine"

18.18 Wolfgang Amadeus Mozart, Piano Sonata, K. 331, mvt. 1

18.19 Joseph Haydn, String Quartet in E♭ Major, Op. 20, No. 1, mvt. 2 (adapted)

18.20 Christian Petzold, Minuet, from the *Anna Magdalena Bach Notebook*

18.21 Ludwig van Beethoven, Symphony No. 8, mvt. 1 (adapted)

18.22 Charlotte Sachsen-Gotha-Altenburg, Canzonette for Keyboard (adapted)

18.23 Franz Schubert's *"Des Müllers Blumen"* ("The Miller's Flowers"), from *Die schöne Mullerin* (adapted)

18.24 Juventino Rosas, *"Sobre las olas"* ("Over the Waves") (adapted)

Ensembles

18.25 Joseph Haydn, String Quartet in G Major, Op. 3, No. 3, mvt. 3
(adapted)

18.26 Ludwig van Beethoven, German Dance No. 3

Sing *le* (♭6̂) for D♭ and *fi* (♯4̂) for B♮.

18.27 Muzio Clementi, Sonatina in G Major, Op. 36, No. 5, Rondo

Play the left hand and sing the melody, or perform as a trio.

18.28 Thomas Morley, "Sing We and Chant It"

Improvisation 18.2: Performing Parallel Periods

1. Sing line 1 to learn the melodic outline of each tune in lines 2-5.
Sing lines 2-5 as individual melodic parts, or improvise a new
variant of the melody by jumping from line to line on each measure
or half measure.

Part II Diatonic Harmony and Tonicization

2. Sing with a partner, alternating phrases, then alternating measures or half measures.

Harmonizing Melodies with Predominant Harmonies

Melodic lines can imply harmony. For example, the line *do-mi-sol* ($\hat{1}$-$\hat{3}$-$\hat{5}$) implies a tonic harmony.

These pitches . . .	Imply the function . . .	And the chord . . .
do, mi, sol ($\hat{1}$-$\hat{3}$-$\hat{5}$)	Tonic (T)	I
fa, la, do ($\hat{4}$-$\hat{6}$-$\hat{1}$)	Predominant (PD)	IV
sol, ti, re, fa ($\hat{5}$-$\hat{7}$-$\hat{2}$-$\hat{4}$)	Dominant (D)	V7

Keyboard 18.3: Performing Phrases with Predominants

Play the progression three times, singing parts 1, 2, and 3, respectively. Then, perform in the parallel minor, remembering to raise the leading tone in chord 5.

- Chords 1–3 work well to begin or continue phrases, or to create a plagal cadence.
- Chords 3–5 create a half cadence.
- Chords 5–6 create a perfect authentic cadence.

Melodies

Use the voice leading from *Keyboard 18.3* to harmonize melodies 18.29–18.34. Play chord 1 and begin singing the melody. Change chords using the rhythm on the single-line staff above each melody.

18.29 Traditional (United States), "Amazing Grace"

18.30 Antonín Dvořák, Symphony No. 9, mvt. 2 (adapted)

18.31 Leopold Mozart, *Burlesque*

18.32 Traditional (Russia), "Over the Distant Lonely Mountains"

18.33 Traditional (England), "The Wassail Bough"

18.34 Traditional (France), "*O ma tendre musette*"
("O My Dear Musette")

Syncopation with Borrowed Beat Divisions

In the following rhythms, syncopation occurs when a borrowed division of the beat is stressed.

Rhythms

18.35

Fast

18.36

Allegretto

18.37

Slowly

18.38

Lively

18.39

Moderato

18.40

Moderato

18.41

Andante

18.42

Calmy

18.48

Duet

18.49

Tonicizing V and Combined Beat Divisions in Simple Meters

CHAPTER 19

In this chapter you'll learn to:

- Perform music that includes secondary dominants and leading-tone chords of V
- Perform simple-meter music with simultaneous compound and simple beat divisions

Tonicizing V

Chromatic pitches can suggest a dominant-tonic relationship that applies to a chord other than I. For example, when fi ($\sharp\hat{4}$) is the leading tone of a dominant-function chord that resolves to V, the chord containing fi ($\sharp\hat{4}$) is called a *secondary dominant*, V is a *secondary tonic*, and V has been *tonicized*.

Melodies

19.1 John Stafford Smith and Francis Scott Key, "The Star-Spangled Banner" (adapted)

19.2 Thomas Ford, "Since First I Saw Your Face"

19.3 John Hook, "The Lass of Richmond Hill" (adapted)

19.4 Charlotte Alington Barnard, "Janet's Choice"

They say I may mar-ry the Laird if I will, the Laird of high de - gree, And jew-els so fair I may twine in my hair, And a La-dy I'd sure - ly be; But Oh! where would my heart be? In

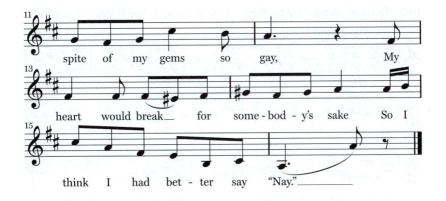

spite of my gems so gay, My heart would break___ for some - bod - y's sake So I think I had bet - ter say "Nay."___

19.5 Felix Mendelssohn, *Volkslied* ("Folksong"), Op. 47, No. 4

Ziemlich langsam

19.6 Maria Lindsay Bliss, "Resignation"

Larghetto

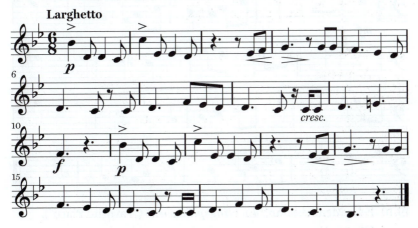

19.7 Richard Strauss, *"Für fünfzehn Pfennige"* ("For Fifteen Pennies")

19.8 Felix Mendelssohn, *"Frühlingslied"* ("Spring Song"), Op. 79, No. 2

19.9 Traditional (England), "Pretty Polly Oliver"

19.10 Felix Mendelssohn, *"Lieblingsplätzchen"* ("Favorite Place"), Op. 99, No. 3

19.11 Carl Reinecke, Polka

19.12 John Liptrot Hatton and William Henry Bellamy,
"Simon the Cellarer" (adapted)

Old Si - mon the cel-lar - er keeps a rare store Of

Malm - sey and Mal - voi - sie,_____ And

Cy - prus, and who can say how ma-ny more! For a

cha - ry old soul is he_____ A

cha - ry old soul_____ is he._____

Sometimes tonicization of V is only implied by the melody, and *fi* (♯4̂) appears in another voice.

19.13 Amy Beach *"Chanson d'amour"* ("Song of Love")

When harmonizing, tonicize the V at the end.

19.14 Johannes Brahms, String Sextet No. 1 in B♭ Major,
     Rondo (cello part)

When harmonizing, try a deceptive resolution in measure 4 and V7/V at the cadence.

19.15 Felix Mendelssohn, *"Wartend"* ("Waiting"), Op. 9, No. 3 (adapted)

19.16 Franz Schubert, *"Mit dem grünen Lautenband"* ("With the Lute's Green Ribbon"), from *Die schöne Müllerin*

Ensembles

19.17 Johannes Brahms, *Liebeslieder Waltzer*, Op. 52, No. 11

19.18 Ludwig van Beethoven, Piano Sonata in G Major, Op. 79, mvt. 3

19.19 Giovanni Battista Pescetti, *Presto* (adapted)

19.20 Ludwig van Beethoven, German Dance No. 6, Trio

19.21 Louise Bertin, *"La Hirondelle"* (adapted)

19.22 Thomas Morley, "Now Is the Month of Maying"

19.23 Johann Sebastian Bach, *"Herr Jesu Christ, dich zu unswend"* ("Lord Jesus Christ, Turn to Us") from *Eighteen Chorale Preludes for Organ*, BWV 655 (adapted)

Harmonizing Melodies That Tonicize the Dominant (V)

Melodic pitches imply harmony. For example, melodic pitch *fi* (♯4̂) implies V7/V.

These pitches . . .	Imply the function . . .	And the chord . . .
do, mi, sol (1̂–3̂–5̂)	Tonic (T)	I
fa, la, do (4̂–6̂–1̂)	Predominant (PD)	IV
sol, ti, re, fa (5̂–7̂–2̂–4̂)	Dominant (D)	V7
fi (♯4̂)	Dominant (D) of V	V7/V

Keyboard and Improvisation 19.1:
Performing Periods That Include Tonicization of V

1. Play the progression and sing the soprano in a comfortable register. Play again while singing an embellishment of the soprano that creates a parallel period or a contrasting period.

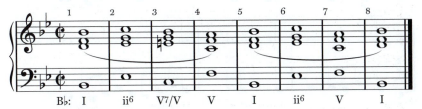

2. Create the following variations:

   a. Person 1 accompanies while person 2 improvises. Switch roles and perform again.

   b. Person 1 improvises the antecedent phrase, and person 2 the consequent.

   c. Vary the musical style (pop song, jazz, and so on). Create rhythmic embellishments in the accompaniment characteristic of the chosen style.

   d. Perform in the parallel minor mode or in a transposed key.

Melodies

Use the voice leading in *Keyboard and Improvisation 19.1* to harmonize melodies 19.24–19.28. Play chord 1 and begin singing the melody. Change chords using the rhythm above the melody. Where no harmonic rhythm is suggested, play V7/V at places indicated with an arrow.

19.25 Traditional (Norway), "*Ranveig*"

19.26 Richard Rodgers and Oscar Hammerstein II, "Climb Ev'ry Mountain," from *The Sound of Music*

Harmonize m. 5 with a minor tonic triad.

19.27 Traditional (Wales), "The Ash Grove"

19.28 Daniel Gottlob Türk, Gavotte (adapted)

Combined Beat Divisions in Simple Meters

In simple meters, compound beat divisions are indicated as triplets. Compound and simple beat divisions can occur simultaneously, creating "three against two" or "two against three" (3:2 or 2:3).

Rhythms

Perform these rhythms as duets or as solos, tapping the right hand and left hand as shown, or tapping the lower part while singing the upper and vice versa.

19.29

19.30

19.31

19.32

19.33

19.34

19.35

19.36

19.37

19.38

19.39

Tonicizing Scale Degrees Other Than $\hat5$, Combined Beat Divisions in Compound Meter, and Harmonizing Melodies That Tonicize the Subdominant

In this chapter you'll learn to:

- Perform, harmonize, and improvise tonicizations of scale degrees other than $\hat5$
- Perform compound-meter rhythms with simultaneous compound and simple beat divisions
- Improvise periods that include secondary dominants of IV

Tonicizing Scale Degrees Other Than $\hat5$

Chromatic pitches often imply tonicization. Raised pitches rise and can sound like *ti* ($\hat7$). Lowered pitches fall and can sound like *fa* ($\hat4$), *le* ($\flat\hat6$), or *ra* ($\flat\hat2$).

Ti ($\hat7$) functions as a diatonic pitch, even though in minor keys it requires an accidental. Thus, "canceling" *ti* ($\hat7$)'s accidental means *te* ($\flat\hat7$) can signal movement away from tonic.

Major keys

If I hear . . .	the chord tonicized is . . .
fi–sol ($\sharp\hat4$–$\hat5$)	V (most common)
si–la ($\sharp\hat5$–$\hat6$)	vi (common)
di–re ($\sharp\hat1$–$\hat2$)	ii (somewhat common)
ri–mi ($\sharp\hat2$–$\hat3$)	iii (rare)
te–la ($\flat\hat7$–$\hat6$)	IV (very common)

Minor keys

If I hear . . .	the chord tonicized is . . .
fi–sol ($\sharp\hat4$–$\hat5$)	V or v (very common)
mi–fa ($\natural\hat3$–$\hat4$)	iv (very common)
te, not *ti* ($\flat\hat7$, not $\hat7$)	III (most common)
te and *ra* ($\flat\hat7$ and $\flat\hat2$)	VI (common)

Melodies

20.1 Felix Mendelssohn, "*Grüß*" ("Greeting"), Op. 19, No. 5

20.2 Traditional (Ireland), "The Minstrel Boy"

20.3 Bart Howard, "Fly Me to the Moon"

Fly me to the moon,_ and let me play a-mong the stars;_

Let me see what spring_ is like on Ju - pi-ter and Mars.__

20.4 Carl Wilhelm, "The Watch on the Rhine"

20.5 Felix Mendelssohn, *"Auf Flügeln des Gesanges"*
("On the Wings of Song"), Op. 34, No. 2

20.6 Fanny Mendelssohn Hensel, Song No. 3 from *Songs for Pianoforte*

20.7 Alexis Lwoff, "Russian National Hymn" (adapted)

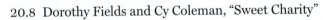

The next melodies feature *te* (♭$\hat{7}$), which tonicizes the subdominant (IV).

20.8 Dorothy Fields and Cy Coleman, "Sweet Charity"

20.9 Franz Schubert, *"Danksgesang an den Bach"* ("Song of Thanks to the Brook"), from *Die schöne Müllerin*

20.10 Richard Rodgers and Oscar Hammerstein II, "It Might as Well Be Spring," from *State Fair*

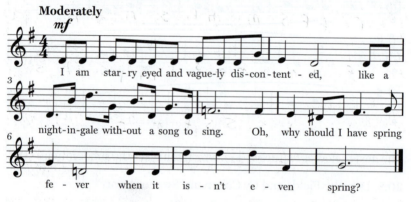

Raised scale degrees can also be chromatic neighbor tones rather than tonicizations.

20.11 Fred Ebb and John Kander, *"Wilkommen,"* from *Cabaret*

20.12 J. Rado, G. Ragni, and G. MacDermot, "Where Do I Go?"

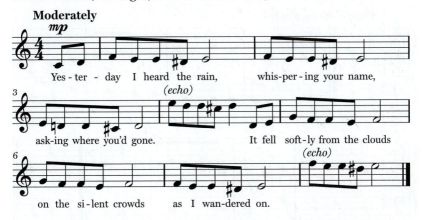

Yes-ter-day I heard the rain, whis-per-ing your name,
(echo)
ask-ing where you'd gone. It fell soft-ly from the clouds
(echo)
on the si-lent crowds as I wan-dered on.

Ensembles

20.13 Johann Sebastian Bach, *Ich liebe Jesum alle Stund*
("I Love Jesus in Every Hour")

20.14 Ludwig van Beethoven, German Dance No. 6, Minuet (adapted)

20.15 Johann Sebastian Bach, *"Nun lob,' mein' Seel,' den Herren"* ("Now Praise My Soul the Lord"), BWV 309

20.16 Johann Sebastian Bach, Bourrée II, from Suite No. 2 for Orchestra (adapted)

20.17 Henry Purcell, "Air" (adapted)

20.18 Johann Sebastian Bach, *"Herr, wie du willst, so schicks mit mir"* ("Lord, Deal with Me as You Wish"), BWV 73

Raised pitches can act as leading tones to the scale degree they tonicize.

20.19 Johann Sebastian Bach, Duet 2, from *Clavierübung* III

20.20 Johann Sebastian Bach, *"Jesus Christus, unser Heiland"* ("Jesus Christ, Our Savior"), from *Eighteen Chorale Preludes for Organ*, BWV 666 (adapted)

Chorale melody

Bach's setting of the chorale melody

20.21 Johann Sebastian Bach, Duet 3, from *Clavierübung* III (adapted)

Harmonizing Melodies That Tonicize the Subdominant (IV)

Melodic pitches imply harmony. For example, melodic pitch *te* ($\flat\hat{7}$) implies V7/IV.

These pitches …	Imply the function …	And the chord …
do, mi, sol ($\hat{1}$–$\hat{3}$–$\hat{5}$)	Tonic (T)	I
fa, la, do ($\hat{4}$–$\hat{6}$–$\hat{1}$)	Predominant (PD)	IV
sol, ti, re, fa ($\hat{5}$–$\hat{7}$–$\hat{2}$–$\hat{4}$)	Dominant (D)	V7
fi ($\sharp\hat{4}$)	Dominant (D) of V	V7/V
te ($\flat\hat{7}$)	Dominant (D) of IV	V7/IV

Keyboard and Improvisation 20.1: Performing Periods That Include Tonicization of IV

1. Play the progression and sing the soprano in a comfortable register. Play again while singing an embellishment of the soprano part that creates a parallel period or a contrasting period.

2. Create the following variations:

   a. Person 1 accompanies while person 2 improvises. Switch roles and perform again.

   b. Person 1 improvises the antecedent phrase, and person 2 the consequent.

   c. Vary the musical style (pop song, jazz, and so on). Create rhythmic embellishments in the accompaniment that are characteristic of the chosen style.

   d. Perform in the parallel minor mode.

   e. Transpose to D major and E♭ major.

3. *Quick Composition:* Notate your favorite improvisation. Include the accidental on *te* (♭$\hat{7}$). Exchange with a peer and sing each other's melody.

Melodies

Use the voice leading in *Keyboard and Improvisation 20.1* to harmonize melodies 20.22-20.23. Play chord 1 and begin singing the melody. Change chords using the rhythm above the melody.

20.22 Traditional (England), "Do Let Me God"

20.23 Friedrich Silcher, *"Sehnsucht"* ("Longing")

Combined Beat Divisions in Compound Meters

In compound meters, simple beat division is indicated as duplets. Compound and simple beat divisions can occur simultaneously, creating "two against three" or "three against two" or (2:3 or 3:2).

Rhythms

Perform these rhythms as duets or as solos, tapping the right hand and left hand as shown, or tapping the lower part while singing the upper and vice versa.

20.24

20.25

20.26

20.27

20.33

Ensemble

Perform three times, switching parts on each repetition.

20.34

Sequences, Hemiola, and Harmonizing Melodies That Tonicize the Submediant

CHAPTER 21

In this chapter you'll learn to:

- Identify, perform, and improvise sequences
- Harmonize melodies that include tonicization of the submediant (vi)
- Perform hemiola in two- and three-part rhythms

Sequences

Sequences repeatedly transpose a unit of music down or up by the same interval and always include at least the beginning of a third repetition. A two-repetition unit that ascends is called *monte* and one that descends is called *fonte*.

Keyboard and Improvisation 21.1: Performing Sequences

1. Choose a sequence. Play all parts while singing part 1. Play again, this time embellishing part 1 with chordal skips, neighbor tones, and passing tones.

2. Repeat exercise 1, but sing and embellish part 2.

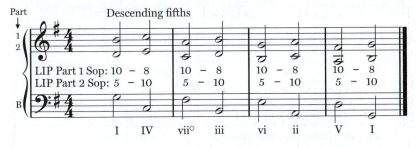

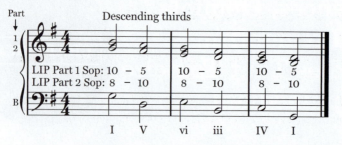

Descending thirds

LIP Part 1 Sop: 10 – 5   10 – 5   10 – 5
LIP Part 2 Sop: 8 – 10   8 – 10   8 – 10

I   V   vi   iii   IV   I

Descending $^6_3$

LIP: 5 – 6   7 – 6   7 – 6   7 – 6   7 – 6   7 – 6   7 – 6   8

I   V7–6   IV7–6   iii7–6   ii7–6   I7–6   vii°7–6   I

Ascending 5–6

LIP: 5 – 6   5 – 6   5 – 6   5 – 6   5 – 6   10

I5–6   ii5–6   iii5–6   IV5–6   V5–6   I

3. Choose a different sequence and repeat the process in exercises 1–2.

4. Perform in other major keys, and in the parallel minor.

Melodies

Using these prompts, *Keyboard and Improvisation 21.1*'s descending fifths sequence can be described this way:

Identify the . . .	to write this sentence . . .
1. key	In the key of G major
2. repeated unit	two-chord units
3. direction	descend
4. interval	by second
5. number of repetitions (reps)	in four reps
6. soprano-bass intervals (linear-intervallic pattern, or LIP)	with a 10-8 LIP.

21.1 Traditional (Germany), "Music Alone Shall Live"
      (round in three parts)

"Melody 21.1 is in F major. In m. 5, two-measure units descend by second in three reps."

This describes a descending-fifth sequence, so from m. 5 to the end, you could harmonize the melody with I–IV–vii°–iii–vi–ii–V–I.

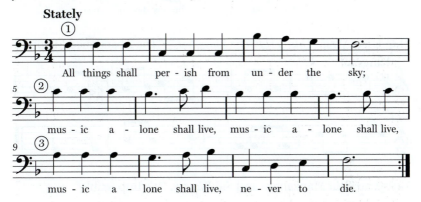

21.2 Élisabeth-Claude Jacquet de la Guerre, Chaconne,
      from *Pièces de clavecin*

21.3 Jackie Rae and James Last, "Happy Heart" (adapted)

21.4 Manos Hadjidakis, "Never on a Sunday" (adapted)

Slow two

f Come an - y day_____ and you'll be my guest,_____ an-y day you say,_____ but my day of rest._____

21.5 Hugo Wolf, *"Das verlassene Mägdlein"* ("The Abandoned Maiden")

Langsam

21.6 Armando Manzanero and Sid Wayne, "It's Impossible"

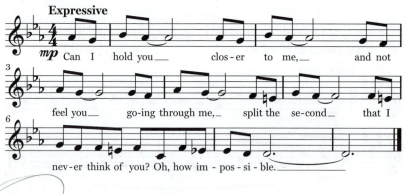

Expressive

mp Can I hold you____ clos - er to me,____ and not feel you____ go-ing through me,____ split the se-cond____ that I nev-er think of you? Oh, how im - pos - si - ble._____

21.7 Norman Gimbel and Charles Fox, "Happy Days"

Allegretto

f Sun - day, Mon - day, Hap-py Days;_ Tues - day, Wednes-day, Hap-py Days,_ Thurs-day, Fri - day, Hap-py Days;_ Sat - ur - day,_ What a day,_

21.8 Maria Theresia von Paradis, Sicilienne (adapted)

21.9 Joseph Haydn, String Quartet in E♭ Major, Op. 50, No. 3, mvt. 1 (adapted)

Allegro con brio

21.10 Franz Schubert, Piano Sonata in G Major, Op. 147, mvt. 3

Allegro giusto

21.11 Jay Livingston and Ray Evans, "Mona Lisa"

Expressive

mf Mo-na Li - sa, Mo-na Li-sa men have named you. You're so

like the la - dy with the mys - tic smile. Is it

on - ly 'cause you're lone-ly___ they have blamed you for that

Mo - na Li - sa strange-ness___ in your smile?

21.12 Ludwig van Beethoven, Kyrie, from *Mass in C*, Op. 86

Andante con moto assai vivace quasi Allegretto ma non troppo

p *cresc. poco a poco*

ff

Ensembles

21.13 Fanny Mendelssohn Hensel, *Notturno in G Minor*

p

21.14 Johann Sebastian Bach, Sonata II, from *Six Trio Sonatas*, BWV 526

21.15 Joseph Haydn, String Quartet in E♭ Major, Op. 50, No. 3, mvt. 2 (adapted)

Andante più tosto Allegretto

21.16 Carl Philipp Emanuel Bach, Sonata in F Major, H. 58 (adapted)

21.17 Joseph Haydn, Piano Sonata No. 33 in D Major, mvt. 3 (adapted)

Tempo di menuetto

21.18 Johann Sebastian Bach, Versus V, from Cantata No. 4,
Christ lag in Todesbanden (*Christ Lay in Death's Bonds*),
BWV 4 (adapted)

21.19 Joseph Haydn, String Quartet in C Major, Op. 20, No. 2, mvt. 3 (adapted)

Menuetto. Allegretto

21.20 Joseph Haydn, String Quartet in E♭ Major, Op. 50, No. 3, mvt. 4 (adapted)

Harmonizing Melodies That Tonicize the Submediant

Chromatic pitch *si* (♯$\hat{5}$) often tonicizes the submediant (vi).

Keyboard and Improvisation 21.2:
Performing a Sequence That Tonicizes vi

1. Play all parts while singing the soprano. Play again, using the soprano pitches as guide tones for singing embellishments like chordal skips, neighbor tones, and passing tones.

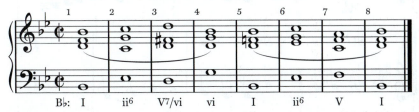

Bb: I   ii⁶   V7/vi   vi   I   ii⁶   V   I

2. Transpose the progression to D and G major. Repeat exercise 1 in each new key.

Melodies

Use the voice leading from *Keyboard and Improvisation 21.2* to harmonize melodies 21.21–21.23. Follow the suggested harmonic rhythm; you may repeat a chord.

21.21 Traditional (England), "The Jolly Waterman"

21.22 Traditional (England), "Love Me Little, Love Me Long"

21.23 Traditional (Italy), *Siciliana*

Hemiola

Six equal note values may divide into two groups of three or three groups of two. When one division prevails, a temporary change to the other creates *hemiola*. Changed beaming or accents can indicate hemiola.

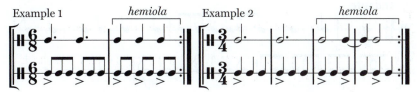

Rhythms

Conduct each rhythm in the meter signature specified, but look for musical cues, like changed beaming, to emphasize the hemiola.

21.25a

Andante

21.25b

Andante

21.26

Allegretto

21.27

Moderato

21.33

21.34

21.35

21.36

21.37

Melodies

21.38 Antonio Vivaldi, "*Domine Fili unigenite*" ("O Lord, Only-begotten Son"), No. 6, from *Gloria* in D major, RV 589

21.39 Johann Sebastian Bach, Fugue in E♭ Major ("St. Anne") BWV 552 (adapted)

This melody concludes on the tonic.

21.40 Traditional (Mexico), *"Mi sueño"* ("My Dream")

21.41 Franz Schubert, *Valse sentimentale*, D. 779, No. 12 (adapted)

21.42 Traditional (Spain), *Peteneras* (Flamenco Song)

Chromaticized Descending-Fifth Sequences

Use accidentals in a descending-fifth sequence to create secondary dominants.

Keyboard and Improvisation 21.3: Performing Chromaticized Descending-Fifth Sequences

1. Perform each sequence *without* the parenthetical accidentals while singing part 1. Perform again while using part 1 as guide tones for singing melodic embellishments.

2. Perform each sequence *with* the parenthetical chromatic pitches while singing part 1. Perform again while using part 1 as guide tones for singing melodic embellishments.

3. Repeat exercises 1–2, but sing part 3.

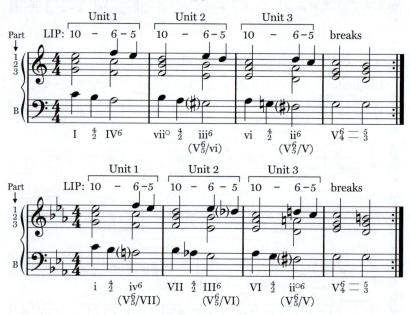

PART III

Chromatic Harmony and Form

Modulation to Closely Related Keys, Harmonizing Melodies That Tonicize the Mediant in Minor, and Changing Meters

CHAPTER 22

In this chapter you'll learn to:

- Perform and improvise music that modulates to closely related keys
- Change solmization when modulating
- Harmonize minor-key melodies that tonicize the mediant
- Perform music that changes meters

Tonicization, Modulation to Closely Related Keys, and Changing Solmization

Tonicization and modulation both use chromatic pitches and secondary dominants, but may be interpreted differently to emphasize their significance.

	How do I decide between them?	*Should I keep or change the solmization?*
Tonicization	Brief, often just a secondary dominant chord or a D–T progression	Keep tonic-key syllables and numbers.
Modulation	More significant, including PD–D or PD–D–T progression and, often, a cadence	You may change to syllables and numbers *in the secondary key.*

Compared with the tonic key, closely related keys have the same key signature or one that differs by only one accidental.

Keyboard and Improvisation 22.1:
Performing Modulations to Closely Related Keys

Link two transpositions of the same progression to modulate from I to the keys of V, vi, and IV.

1. Perform and memorize chords 1–5, a key-establishing progression.

2. Transpose chords 1–5 to destination keys G major (V), A minor (vi), and F major (IV).

3. Link the progressions using an incomplete V7 in the chosen destination key. Bent brackets show that I pivots to become IV in the destination key. Change the solmization at or near the pivot chord.

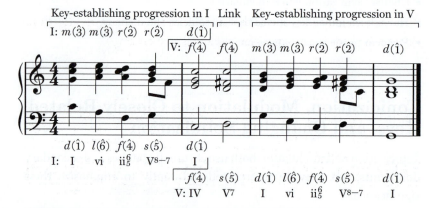

4. Choose a modulation as the basis for an improvised recitative. Sustain each chord and sing melodic embellishments of the soprano part.

Follow the same procedure to modulate from i to the keys of v, VI, iv, and III.

5. Perform chords 1–5 in the parallel minor. *Ti* ($\hat{7}$) requires an accidental.

6. Transpose chords 1–5 to these destination keys:
   (a) G minor (v)   (b) A♭ major (VI)
   (c) F minor (iv)   (d) E♭ major (III)

7. For exercises 6 (a)–(c), link as before, using an incomplete V7 in the destination key.

For 6 (d), use this new link. This link works for the other modulations, too.

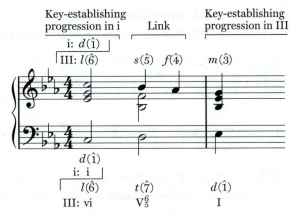

Melodies

Scan each melody. Decide whether it includes tonicization, modulation, or both. If there is a modulation, change the solmization.

22.1 Maria Lindsay Bliss, "Tired"

22.2 Emilie Mayer, *"O lass mich dein gedenken"* ("O, Let Me Remember You"), Op. 7, No. 2

22.3 Johannes Brahms, *"Die Wollust in den Maien"* ("Springtime Sensuality"), from *28 Deutsche Volkslieder*, WoO 32

22.4 Felix Mendelssohn, *"Jagdlied"* ("Hunting Song"), Op. 84, No. 3

22.5 Felix Mendelssohn, *"Das erste Veilchen"* ("The First Violets"), Op. 19, No. 2

22.6 Amy Beach, *"Ariette"*

22.7 Johann Sebastian Bach, *"Auf, auf, mein Herz, mit Freuden"*
      ("Awake, My Heart, with Gladness"), BWV 441

The next four melodies include modulations to V.

22.8 Friedrich Silcher, *"Hoffe das Beste"* ("Hope for the Best")

22.9 Johann Sebastian Bach, No. 13 from *St. John Passion* (adapted)

22.10 Elisabetta de Gambarini, March, Op. 1, No. 4 (adapted)

22.11 Johannes Brahms, String Sextet No. 1, mvt. 4 (adapted)

22.12 Johann Sebastian Bach, Cello Suite No. 1 in G Major, Courante

The next six melodies include modulations to v.

22.13 Felix Mendelssohn, *Erntelied* ("Harvest Song"), Op. 8, No. 4

22.14 Fanny Mendelssohn Hensel, *Schwanenlied* ("Swan Song"),
from *Six Songs*, Op. 1, No. 1

22.15 Wolfgang Amadeus Mozart, Symphony No. 40, K. 550,
Menuetto (adapted)

22.16 Felix Mendelssohn, String Quartet in E♭ Major, Op. 12, mvt. 4

22.17 Felix Mendelssohn, *"Pagenlied"* ("The Page's Song") (adapted)

22.18 Felix Mendelssohn, *"Suleika,"* Op. 34, No. 4 (adapted)

The next four melodies include modulations to III.

22.19 George Frideric Handel, Suite in D Minor, Gigue

22.20 Robert Schumann, *"Sheherazade,"* from *Album for the Young,* Op. 68, No. 25 (adapted)

Ziemlich langsam, leise

22.21 Fanny Mendelssohn Hensel, *"Schöne Fremde"*
("Beautiful Stranger"), Op. 3, No. 2

22.22 Henry Purcell, "Or If More Influencing to Brisk,"
from *Rosy Bow'rs*

Ensembles

22.23 Ludwig van Beethoven, String Quartet, Op. 132,
     mvt. 5 (adapted)

Allegro appassionato

22.24 Fanny Mendelssohn Hensel, Suite in F♯ Minor, G. 207,
     Gigue (adapted)

22.25 Ludwig van Beethoven, Piano Sonata in A♭ Major, Op. 110, mvt. 1 (adapted)

22.26 Robert Schumann, *"Fremder Mann"* ("The Stranger"), from
Album for the Young, Op. 68, No. 29 (adapted)

22.27 Ludwig van Beethoven, Piano Sonata in F Minor, Op. 2, No. 1,
mvt. 3 (adapted)

Harmonizing Melodies That Tonicize the Mediant in Minor Keys

Minor-key music usually includes *ti* ($\hat{7}$). A change to *te* ($\flat\hat{7}$) can imply tonicization of III because *te* ($\flat\hat{7}$) is the root of V7/III.

Keyboard and Improvisation 22.2:
Tonicizing the Minor-Key Mediant

1. Play the progression and sing the soprano part. Play again. Use the soprano part as guide tones and sing an improvisation.

2. Use the progression's chords and voice leading to harmonize melodies 22.28–22.30. Play chord 1, begin singing the melody, and change to chords that include the melodic pitch.

Keyboard and improvisation progression

a: i   V⁶   i   V7/III   III   iv   V   i

Melodies

22.28 Johann Sebastian Bach, Chorale 285, *"Wär Gott nicht mit uns diese Zeit"* ("If God Were Not with Us at This Time")

a: V7/III III

22.29 Johann Sebastian Bach, Chorale 301, *"Ach, lieben Christen, seid getrost"* ("Ah, Dear Christians, Be Comforted")

g: V7/III III

22.30 Johann Sebastian Bach, Chorale 336, *"Wo Gott Herr nicht bei uns Hält"* ("If the Lord God Does Not Stay with Us")

b: V7/III III

Changing Meters

Typically, changing meter occurs in two ways.

	Example	What stays the same	What changes
Beat-unit equivalence	‖ ¾ |4⁄4 |2⁄4 |	Beat unit and duration	Beat grouping
Note-value equivalence	♪=♪ ‖ 6⁄8 |2⁄4 |	One note value	Beat duration

Rhythms

Keep the beat steady, but change the conducting pattern with each meter change.

22.31

22.32

22.33

22.34

22.35

Tap eighth notes and perform, emphasizing the metrical accents. Perform again and conduct, changing the beat duration when the meter changes.

22.36

22.37

22.38

22.39

Rhythmic Ensembles

22.40

22.41

Melodies

22.42 Johannes Brahms, *Variations on a Hungarian Song*, Op. 21, No. 2

22.43 Traditional (England), "Shanadar"

Shan - a - dar is a rol - ling ri - ver, E -
o,___ e - o,___ e - o,___ e - o.___

22.44 Jim Webb, "Galveston"

Gal - ves-ton,___ oh, Gal - ves - ton,
I still hear___ your sea_____ winds___ blow-ing,___

22.45 Traditional (England), "The Rejected Lover"

O once I knew a pret-ty girl, and I loved her as my
life; And I'd free - ly give my heart and hand to
make her my wife, O_____ to make her my wife.

22.46 Gustav Mahler, Symphony No. 2, mvt. 5 (adapted)

22.47 Traditional (Germany), *"Mädle, ruck, ruck, ruck"*
("Maiden, Come Sit by My Side")

22.48 Pyotr Ilyich Tchaikovsky, String Quartet in F Major, Op. 22,
Scherzo (adapted)

Melodic Ensemble

22.49 Hans Leo Hassler, *"Mein G'müth ist mir verwirret"*
 ("My Mind Is Confused")

Binary and Ternary Forms, Modulation to Closely Related Keys in Minor, and Changing Meter with Beat-Duration Equivalence

CHAPTER 23

In this chapter you'll learn to:

- Perform music in binary and ternary form
- Improvise minor-key music that modulates to closely related keys
- Perform changing meter with beat-duration equivalence

Binary, Ternary, and Composite Form

Form is the product of a piece's harmonic structure and melodic design. Two-part forms are called binary. Each section may repeat (or "reprise"). Traditional dances, like minuets and trios, and many folk songs are in binary form. Several terms distinguish binary form types.

Is the binary form . . .	Choose option 1 if . . .	Choose option 2 if . . .
(1) rounded or (2) simple?	section 2 ends with a recap of section 1.	there is no recap of section 1.
(1) sectional or (2) continuous?	section 1 ends with a PAC in I (or i).	section 1 ends any any other way.
balanced, (1) yes or (2) no?	both sections conclude similarly.	the sections end differently.

Ternary form comprises three sections: **A B A**. Often, the **B** section is its own key. Ternary form works include *da capo* arias and minuet-and-trio movements. In the latter, each ternary-form section is itself a binary dance. Form within form is called composite form.

Melodies

23.1 Robert Schumann, *"Trällerliedchen"* ("Humming Song"), from *Album for the Young*, Op. 68, No. 3 (adapted)

23.2 Traditional (Poland), "Little Cottage Lowly" (Mazurka)

23.3 Traditional (Sweden), *"Wermeland"*

23.4 Mrs. E. Fitzgerald, "I Remember, I Remember" (adapted)

23.5 Edvard Grieg, String Quartet in G Minor, Op. 27, mvt. 3 (adapted)

23.6 Robert Schumann, *"Wichtige Begebenheit"* ("Important Event"), from *Scenes from Childhood*, Op. 15, No. 6 (adapted)

23.7 Wolfgang Amadeus Mozart, String Quartet in B♭ Major, K. 458, Menuetto (adapted)

23.8 Traditional (Spain), *Canción de Maja* ("Song of a Young Lady")

23.9 Walter Kittredge, "Tenting on the Old Camp Ground"

23.10 Sophie de Zybine, "*Si tu le vois*" ("If You See Him") (adapted)

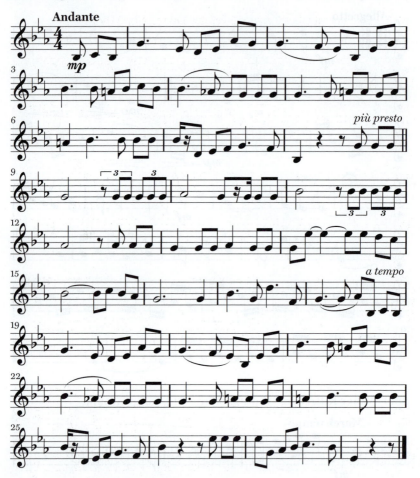

Ensembles

23.11 Ludwig van Beethoven, German Dance No. 2 (adapted)

23.12 Henry Purcell, Minuet (adapted)

23.13 Élisabeth-Claude Jacquet de la Guerre, Suite in D Minor, Rigadoun II (adapted)

23.14 Wolfgang Amadeus Mozart, Clarinet Quintet, K. 581, mvt. 4 (adapted)

Modulations to Closely Related Keys in Minor

Modulations in minor keys use the same principles as those in major. However, the minor mode typically modulates to different destination keys.

Keyboard and Improvisation 23.1: Performing Modulations to Closely Related Keys in Minor

Link transpositions of the same progression to modulate from i to the keys of v, VI, iv, and III.

1. Perform and memorize chords 1–5, a key-establishing progression.

2. Transpose chords 1–5 to these destination keys:

   (a) G minor (v) (b) Ab major (VI)

   (c) F minor (iv) (d) Eb major (III)

3. Link progressions 6 (a)–(c) using an incomplete V7 in the chosen destination key. Bent brackets show that I pivots to become iv in the destination key. Change the solmization at or near the pivot chord.

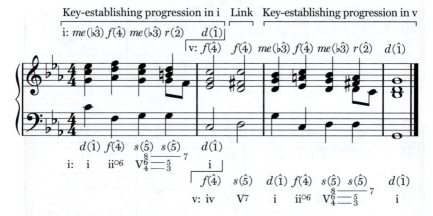

4. To modulate from i to III, use this link. This link works with the other modulations, too.

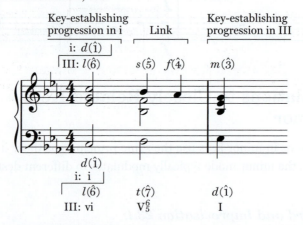

5. Choose a modulation as the basis for an improvised recitative. Sustain each chord and sing melodic embellishments of the soprano part.

6. *Quick Composition:* Notate an improvisation and exchange it with a peer. Sing and critique each other's music.

Ensembles

23.15 Henry Purcell, "A Farewell" (adapted)

23.16 Daniel Gottlob Türk, "Evening Song"

23.17 Ludwig van Beethoven, String Trio in D Major, Op. 9, No. 2, mvt. 2 (adapted)

Changing Meter

In addition to beat-unit equivalence and note-value equivalence, changing meter can occur as beat-duration equivalence.

	Example	What stays the same	What changes
Beat-unit	‖ $\frac{3}{4}$ | $\frac{4}{4}$ | $\frac{2}{4}$ |	beat unit and duration	beat grouping
Note-value	‖ $\frac{6}{8}$ ♪=♪ | $\frac{2}{4}$ |	one note value	beat duration
Beat duration	‖ $\frac{6}{8}$ ♩.=♩ | $\frac{2}{4}$ |	beat duration	beat unit and division

Rhythms

Rhythms 23.18a and 23.18b sound identical. Conduct them in duple meter, keeping the beat duration the same throughout.

23.18a

23.18b

23.28

Melodies

23.29 Traditional (Jamaica), "Dry-Bone"

23.30 Samuel Coleridge-Taylor, "Song of Conquest," Op. 59, No. 5

23.31 Edvard Grieg, *"En Konge hersked I Österland"* ("A King Ruled in the East"), from *Norwegian Folk Songs*, Op. 66, No. 3

23.32 Traditional (England), "Bean Setting" (Stick Dance)

23.33 Edvard Grieg, *"Guten Aa Gjenta paa Fjøshjellen"* ("The Lad and the Lass in the Cow-Shed Loft"), from *Six Norwegian Mountain Melodies*, No. 6

23.34 Pyotr Ilyich Tchaikovsky, The Sleeping Beauty, Act 2, No. 15a, "The Vision" (adapted)

Contrapuntal Practices and Dual Meter Signatures

CHAPTER 24

In this chapter you'll learn to:

- Realize figured bass notation to improvise a binary-form composition
- Perform chordal homophony and imitative and nonimitative polyphony
- Perform changing-meter rhythms notated with dual meter signatures
- Transpose, invert, and sequence motives

Realizing Figured Bass

Figured bass is a musical shorthand. Unless there are alterations, play key-signature pitches. Here are common figured bass symbols and alterations.

Type	Symbol	Abbreviation	Over a left hand bass pitch, use key-signature pitches and play in the right hand . . .
Triad	$\frac{5}{3}$		a root-position triad
	$\frac{6}{3}$	6	a first-inversion triad
	$\frac{6}{4}$	$\frac{6}{4}$	a second-inversion triad
Seventh	$\frac{7}{3}$	7	a root-position seventh chord
	$\frac{6}{5}$	$\frac{6}{5}$	a first-inversion seventh chord
	$\frac{6}{4}{3}$	$\frac{4}{3}$	a second-inversion seventh chord
	$\frac{6}{4}{2}$	$\frac{4}{2}$	a third-inversion seventh chord

Alteration	Example	Over the bass pitch . . .
‿	6̸	raise the 6th
♯	♯	raise the 3rd
+	+4	raise the 4th
♭	♭6	lower the 6th
♮	♮3	play a "natural" 3rd

Keyboard and Improvisation 24.1:
Realizing Figured Bass

This bass line comprises a complete binary-form composition. The treble staff shows one of many possible realizations using progressions you know.

1. Perform the bass line. Then, play the realization.

2. Play the realization and sing the soprano part.

3. Play and sing again, embellishing the soprano part with, for example, consonant skips and neighbor tones. Accompany a peer as they embellish the soprano part.

4. Create your own realization of the figured bass. Accompany a peer as they improvise a soprano part.

Chordal Homophony

Chordal homophony is the texture of chorales, hymns, and carols. The parts move in essentially the same rhythm, but the outer-voice contour is contrasting.

Ensembles

Compare the outer voices of Bach's chorales, shown here as two-voice counterpoint. The figured bass is not Bach's, but another possibility that uses what you know.

24.1 Johann Sebastian Bach, *"Brunnquell aller Güter"*
("Fountain of All Good Things")

24.2 Johann Sebastian Bach, *"Auf, auf! Die rechte Zeit ist hier"*
(Up, Up! The Right Time Is Here")

24.3 Johann Sebastian Bach, *"Jesu, deine Liebeswunden"*
("Jesus, Your Dear Wounds")

These chorales include all four parts. Analyze them and re-create the
figured bass.

24.4 Johann Sebastian Bach, *"Jesu, meine Freude"*
("Jesus, My Joy"), BWV 227 (adapted)

24.5 Orlando di Lasso, *Matona mi acara* (My Dear Lady)

Imitative Polyphony

Two or more parts with contrasting rhythm and contour create polyphony. Often, polyphonic music is imitative, meaning parts follow the melody of a leading part, producing a copy of it. Canons and rounds, inventions, and fugues are among the many polyphonic genres.

Ensembles

In rounds and canons, aligning the entrances reveals the counterpoint.

24.6 William Billings, "Babylon" (round in three parts)

24.7 Traditional (France), "Are You Sleeping?" (round in four parts)

24.8 Robert Schumann, *"Canonisches Liedchen"* ("Canonic Song"), from *Album for the Young*, Op. 68, No. 27 (adapted)

24.9 Giovanni Pierluigi da Palestrina, *"Alleluia tulerunt Dominum"* (adapted)

24.10 Johann Sebastian Bach, *"Dir, dir, Jehovah, will ich singen"*
("To You, Jehovah, Will I Sing")

24.11 Johann Sebastian Bach, Invention 6 in E Major, BWV 777
(adapted)

24.12 Ludwig van Beethoven, Piano Sonata in A♭ Major, Op. 110, Fugue (adapted)

Allegro ma non troppo

24.13 Ludwig van Beethoven, Gloria, from *Mass in C*, Op. 86

24.14 Johann Sebastian Bach, *"Der aber die Herzen forschet"* ("He, However, Who Examines Hearts"), from *Der Geist hilft unser Schwachheit auf*, BWV 226 (adapted)

Nonimitative Polyphony

In nonimitative polyphony, parts contrast in rhythm and contour but none is a copy of another.

Ensembles

In exercises 24.16 and 24.17 sing *ra* for ♭$\hat{2}$.

24.16 Johann Sebastian Bach, Recitativo, from Cantata No. 51, *Jauchzet Gott in allen Landen* (*Praise God in All Lands*), BWV 51 (adapted)

Translation: Yet feeble praise can still please Him.

24.17 Johann Sebastian Bach, Agnus Dei, from *Mass in B Minor*

24.18 Johann Sebastian Bach, Et Spiritum Sanctum Dominum,
from *Mass in B Minor*

Melodies can imply multipart voice leading. This is called compound melody.

24.19 Johann Sebastian Bach, Courante, from Violin Partita No. 1 in B Minor

Soloist performs these implied guide tones.

Bach's violin melody.

Play or sing Bach's implied harmonies.

D maj.

Dual Meter Signatures

Dual meter signatures indicate recurring changes of meter.

Rhythms

24.20

24.27

24.28

24.29 Joaquín Rodrigo, *Concierto de Aranjuez*, mvt. 1 (adapted)

24.30

24.31

Melodies

24.32 Joaquín Rodrigo, *Concierto de Aranjuez*, mvt. 3 (adapted)

24.33 Traditional (United States), "The True Lover's Farewell"

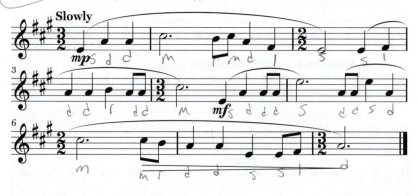

24.34 Traditional (England), "Young Hunting"

Light you down, light you down, love— Hen— ry, she said, And stay all— night with me; For I have a bed and a fire-side too,—— And a can - dle a - burn - ing bright.

24.35 Traditional (United States), "The Rejected Lover"

O once I knew a pret-ty girl, and I loved her as my life; And I'd free - ly give my heart and hand— to make— her my wife, O———— to make— her my wife.

She took me by the hand— and she— led me to the door; And she put her arms a - round me, say-ing you can't come a - ny-more, O———— you can't come a - ny - more.

24.36 Traditional (United States), "Locks and Bolts"

24.37 Traditional (Catalonia), *"La nit de Nadal"* ("Christmas Eve")

Transforming Motives

Motivic transformation can be achieved through transposition, inversion, and sequencing, as well as other approaches such as rhythmic alteration.

Keyboard 24.2: Transforming a Motive

The motive (1) from Bach's Invention No. 1 can be broken down into a head (2) and tail (3). Perform all 3. Then, create the specified transformations.

1. Invention 1 motive (m. 1)   2. Head (fragment)   3. Tail (fragment)

4. Transpose the motive to the dominant pitch (m. 2)

5. Invert the motive from A5 (m. 3).

6. Begin with E4 and invert the tail (m. 5)

7. Begin with E4 and sequence the inverted tail in three rising units (m. 5). Conclude on D5 (m. 6).

8. Begin with B3 and rhythmically augment the head (m. 3).

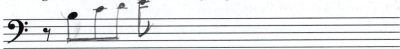

9. Copy (5) into the treble staff and (8) into the bass staff. Then, create a sequence that descends by thirds in two additional units (mm. 3-4).

10. From the given pitches, transpose (9) to D minor. Put (9)'s treble part in the bass clef and vice versa, demonstrating invertible counterpoint. Then, create a sequence that descends by thirds in three units (mm. 11-12).

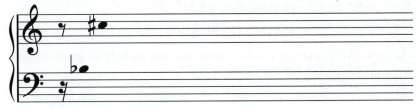

Variations and Super-Subdivided Simple Beats

CHAPTER 25

In this chapter you'll learn to:

- Improvise continuous variations over a ground bass
- Perform a theme and sectional variations of that theme
- Perform simple-meter rhythms with subdivided subdivisions

Continuous Variations

Continuous variations feature a short, repeated pattern over which melodic variations occur. Historically, these pieces had many names. Today, we use these terms:

Term	What is repeated
Passacaglia, ground bass, or thorough bass	bass line
Chaconne	harmonic progression

Keyboard and Improvisation 25.1: Performing Variations over the Lament Bass

1. *Solo:* While playing the keyboard, use the melody as guide tones and sing an improvisation.

2. *Duet:* One person plays while the other sings. Switch roles and perform again.

3. *Trio:* Each person chooses a part; the person singing the melody should embellish it. Repeat and switch parts until everyone has performed all parts.

Very slow and expressive

e: i   10-10 LIP ——————————— V   VI ii⁰⁶ V   i

4. *Quick Composition:* Collaborate within your trio to notate your favorite melodic improvisation. Give your score to a different trio to use as a sight-singing ensemble piece.

Melodies

Repeat each ground bass continuously. Over it, improvise melodic variations.

25.1 Johann Pachelbel, *Ciaconna* in D Major, DdT. v2/1, No. 15

Andante

25.2 Johann Pachelbel, *Ciaconna* in D Major, DdT. v2/1, No. 16

Grazioso

25.3 Johann Pachelbel, *Ciaconna* in D Major, DdT. v2/1, No. 17

Grave

25.4 Johann Sebastian Bach, *Passacaglia* in C Minor for Organ

Maestoso

25.5 Johann Sebastian Bach, *Art of the Fugue*, Contrapunctus I (adapted)

Stately

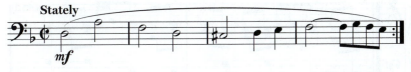

25.6 Henry Purcell, ground bass from "Ground in Gamut," from *Musick's Hand-Maid*

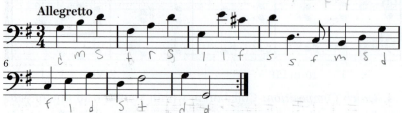

25.7 and 25.9 are well-known chromatic lament basses.

25.7 Henry Purcell, "Dido's Lament," from *Dido and Aeneas* (adapted)

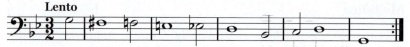

25.8 Henry Purcell, ground bass from "A New Ground," from *Musick's Hand-Maid* (adapted)

Ensembles

25.9 Johann Sebastian Bach, Crucifixus, from *Mass in B Minor* (adapted)

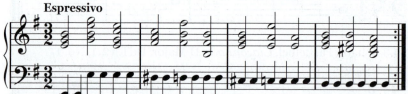

25.10 Johann Pachelbel, *Ciaconna* in C Major, DdT. v2/1, No. 14 (adapted)

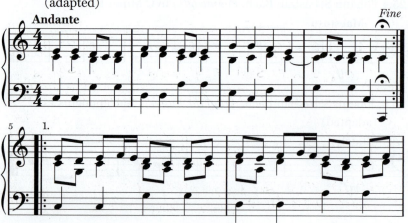

D.C. al Fine

Sectional Variations (Theme and Variations)

Sectional variations begin with a theme followed by a set of variations. Each variation copies the theme's structure, but changes aspects like figuration, style, or texture. Compositions and movements comprising sectional variations have been common since the Classical period.

Melodies

Compare themes by Clara Schumann and Johannes Brahms with some of their variations.

25.11 Clara Schumann, *Variations on a Theme by Robert Schumann*

(a) Theme

(b) Variation 3

(c) Variation 6

25.12 Johannes Brahms, *Variations on an Original Theme for Piano,* Op. 21, No. 1

(a) Theme

(b) Variation 2

(c) Variation 3

(d) Variation 4

Ensembles

25.13 Ludwig van Beethoven, *Variations for Piano*, Op. 76 (adapted)

(a) Theme (adapted)

(b) Variation 1 (adapted)

(c) Variation 3 (adapted)

Super-Subdivided Simple Beats

Super-subdivided beats divide beat subdivisions.

Rhythms

First, tap the beat divisions. Then, conduct the usual beat pattern, but include slight pulses on each beat division.

25.22

Rhythmic Ensembles

25.23

25.24

Melodies

25.25 Franz Schubert, *"Idens Nachtgesang"* ("Ida's Night Song"), D. 227

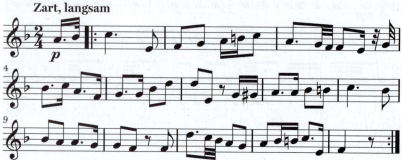

25.26 Wolfgang Amadeus Mozart, Piano Sonata in C Major, K. 309, mvt. 2

25.27 Ludwig van Beethoven, Piano Sonata in C Major, Op. 2, No. 3, mvt. 2 (adapted)

25.28 Carlo Paessler, Largo No. 4 for Oboe (adapted)

25.29 Franz Schubert, *"Des Mädchens Klage"*
("The Girl's Complaint"), D. 191

Melodic Ensemble

25.30 Ludwig van Beethoven, String Trio in D Major, Op. 9, No. 2,
mvt. 2 (adapted)

Figural Variation

Figural variations feature a specific embellishment pattern—or figure—throughout.

Keyboard and Improvisation 25.2: Performing Figural Variations

Use the progression in exercise 1 as the basis for a theme and two variations.

1. Perform the realization. Then play again, improvising simple embellishments of the soprano part.

2. Notate your favorite improvisation. It is the theme you will vary.

3. Create a figural variation. Choose an embellishment (e.g., lower neighbor) and apply it to each pitch of your theme. Notate the variation.

4. Choose a different melodic embellishment and repeat exercise 3.

Modal Mixture and Super-Subdivided Compound Beats

CHAPTER 26

In this chapter you'll learn to:

- Improvise phrases with pitches borrowed from the parallel minor key
- Perform melodies that borrow pitches from the parallel mode
- Perform super-subdivided compound beats

Modal Mixture

Modal mixture borrows pitches or chords from the parallel key. Often, major-key music borrows from its parallel minor.

Keyboard and Improvisation 26.1: Improvising Predominant Chords with Modal Mixture

1. Play the progression twice, the first time in major, the second with the parenthetical ♭6̂, which creates mixture. As you play, sing each part as written.

2. Choose a single embellishment, like a neighbor tone or a chordal skip, and embellish each soprano pitch with it.

3. Combine different embellishments to improvise new, original phrases.

First time: I   IV   ii⁶   V⁶₄—⁵₃   I   IV   ii⁶   V⁶₄—⁵₃   I
Second time: I   iv   ii°⁶   V⁶₄—⁵₃   I   iv   ii°⁶   V⁶₄—⁵₃   I

4. *Quick Composition:* Notate your favorite improvisation as a solo over a four-part choral score. Vertically align the rhythm of all parts. Perform the work as an ensemble piece.

Melodies

26.1 Johannes Brahms, String Sextet No. 2 in G Major, mvt. 1 (adapted)

26.2 Giuseppe Verdi, "*Un dì, felice, eterea*" ("One Day, Happy, Ethereal"), from *La Traviata* (adapted)

26.3 Gustav Mahler, "*In diesem Wetter*" ("In this Weather"), from *Kindertotenlieder*

26.4 Johannes Brahms, *Liebeslieder Waltzer*, Op. 52, No. 3 (adapted)

26.5 Gustav Mahler, "*Die zwei blauen Augen von meinem Schatz*" ("The Two Blue Eyes of My Sweetheart"), from *Lieder eines fahrenden Gesellen* (adapted)

26.6 Dan Fogelberg, "Longer"

26.7 Ludwig van Beethoven, *"Aus Goethes Faust"* ("From Goethe's *Faust*"), No. 3 from *Sechs Gesänge*, Op. 75

26.8 Johannes Brahms, *Intermezzo* in E♭ Major, Op. 117, No. 1

26.9 Johannes Brahms, Piano Sonata No. 1 in C Major, mvt. 1 (adapted)

26.10 Felix Mendelssohn, *Neue Liebe* ("New Love"), Op. 19, No. 4

26.11 Elton John and Bernie Taupin, "Your Song"

Ballad

If I were a sculp-tor___ but then a-gain no,___ or a man who makes po - tions in a trav-el - in' show,___ I know_ it's not much but it's_ the best I can do,___ my gift_ is my song and___ this one's for you._

26.12 Ludwig van Beethoven, *"Lustig, traurig"* ("Funny, Sad"), WoO 43 (adapted)

Lustig

mp   *cresc.*   *Fine*   *D.C. al Fine*

Ensembles

26.13 Johannes Brahms, *Liebeslieder Waltzer*, Op. 65, No. 14 (adapted)

26.14 Gustav Mahler, Symphony No. 2, mvt. 4 (arr. David Geary)

Staff 3 uses a modern tenor clef. Its pitches sound one octave lower than written.

Keyboard and Improvisation 26.2: Modal Mixture

1. Use the given progression to create phrases that employ modal mixture. Begin with chord 1. Performing from left to right, choose one option for each number. For example, play chords 1-2b-3b-4a-5a. Then, play chords 1-2a-3a-4b-5c; and so on. Adjust the rhythms as needed to create complete measures.

2. While playing your progression, use part 1 as guide tones for singing melodic embellishments. Perform again, embellishing part 2 or part 3.

3. Work in pairs. One person performs, while the partner listens and then plays, sings, or notates what was performed. Switch roles.

Super-Subdivided Compound Beats

Dividing subdivided compound-meter beats creates super-subdivided beats. These usually occur during slow tempos. Even so, the beats must retain the feel of a pulse that divides into three.

Rhythms

Conduct the beat divisions as indicated. Emphasize the ♩. beat, and place the beat divisions to the side of each beat.

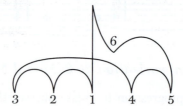

26.15

26.16

Einfach

26.17

Langsam

26.18

26.19

26.20

26.21

Conduct in nine or twelve as indicated.

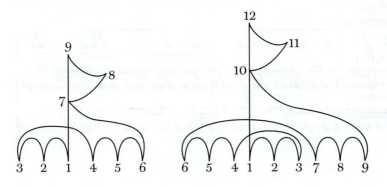

26.22

Ensembles

26.26

26.27

26.28

Melodies

26.29 Ludwig van Beethoven, Septet for Winds, Op. 20, mvt. 2 (adapted)

26.30 Joseph Haydn, Symphony No. 48 in C major, Hob. I:48, mvt. 2
(adapted)

26.31 George Frideric Handel, "Farewell, Ye Limpid Springs and Floods," from *Jephthah* (adapted)

26.32 Joseph Haydn, Symphony No. 57 in D Major, Hob. I:57, mvt. 2 (adapted)

CHAPTER 27

The Neapolitan Sixth, Augmented-Sixth Chords, and Traditional Dance Rhythms

In this chapter you'll learn to:

- Perform and improvise music that includes the Neapolitan sixth (N6) and augmented-sixth (A6) chords
- Perform rhythms characteristic of traditional dances
- Improvise a waltz that includes both N6 and A6 chords

The Neapolitan Sixth (N6)

Three minor-key predominant triads use identical voice leading but differ by one pitch: *do* ($\hat{1}$) in iv, *re* ($\hat{2}$) in ii°6, or *ra* ($\flat\hat{2}$) in the Neapolitan sixth (N6).

Keyboard and Improvisation 27.1: Performing Predominant Triads, including N6

1. Perform chord 1 while singing part 1. Choose and perform a PD chord: 2a, b, or c. Perform or omit chord 3. Perform either 4a ➜ 4b or just 4b. Repeat the process, this time performing part 3 up one octave. Follow this procedure to create other voicings and progressions. However, avoid a part-2 soprano with N6 because it produces P5-P5.

2. Perform again, this time using part 1 as guide tones for improvising melodic embellishments. Repeat the process, using part 3 as the basis for your improvisation.

Melodies

In 27.1–27.2, sustain the stems-down pitches on the keyboard while singing each melody.

27.1

27.2

27.3 Constance Faunt Le Roy, "A Merry Life"

27.4 Hector Berlioz, *Grande symphonie*, Op. 15, mvt. 1

27.5 Felix Mendelssohn, *"Des Mädchens Klage"*
("The Maiden's Lament")

27.6 Johannes Brahms, *Liebeslieder Walzer*, Op. 65, No. 9

27.7 Jack Gold and John Barry, "Midnight Cowboy"

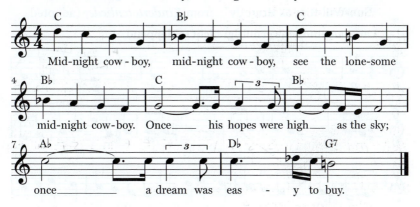

Mid-night cow-boy, mid-night cow-boy, see the lone-some mid-night cow-boy. Once___ his hopes were high___ as the sky; once___ a dream was eas - y to buy.

27.8 John Barry and Don Black, "Thunderball"

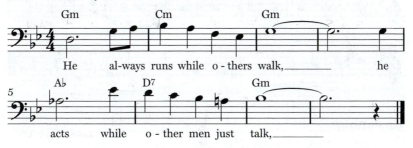

He al-ways runs while o - thers walk,___ he acts while o - ther men just talk,___

27.9 Stephen Schwartz, "Turn Back, O Man"

Built while_ they dream, and in that dream-ing weep, still will not hear___ thine in-ner God pro - claim,

27.10 Gustav Mahler, *"Nun will die Sonn' so hell aufgeh'n"* ("Now the Sun Will Rise as Brightly"), from *Kindertotenlieder* (adapted)

Langsam und schwermütig; nicht schleppend

Ensembles

27.11 Johann Sebastian Bach, Badinerie, from Suite No. 2 for Orchestra, BWV 1067 (adapted)

27.12 Johann Sebastian Bach, Gigue, from Partita No. 3 in A Minor, BWV 827 (adapted in C minor)

Augmented Sixth (A6) Chords

Phrygian resolutions approach the dominant pitch from neighbor tones below and above: $\hat{4}$-$\hat{5}$ and $\hat{6}$-$\hat{5}$. Augmented-sixth chords (A6) chromaticize the Phrygian resolution: $\sharp\hat{4}$-$\hat{5}$ and $\hat{6}$-$\hat{5}$.

Keyboard and Improvisation 27.2: Performing Augmented-Sixth (A6) Chords

1. Perform chord 1 while singing part 1. Choose and perform a PD chord—2a, b, c, or d. Perform either 3a ➔ 3b or just 3b. Repeat the process, taking parts 2 or 3 up one octave to become the melody. Follow this procedure to create other examples. Gr^{+6} can resolve

to V despite the P5–P5. Mozart wrote these characteristic parallel fifths so often they are called "Mozart fifths."

2. Perform again, this time using part 1 as guide tones for improvising melodic embellishments. Repeat the process, using parts 2 and 3 as the basis for melodic improvisations.

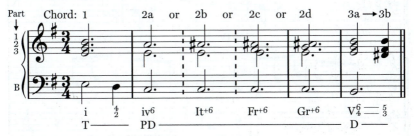

Ensembles

In 27.14 and 27.15, sustain the stems-down pitches on the keyboard while singing or sing with a partner. Then, sing the melody while playing the bass line.

27.14 Gr+6

27.15 Fr+6

27.16 Johann Sebastian Bach, Kyrie, from *Mass in B Minor*

27.17 Ludwig van Beethoven, *Eleven Bagatelles*, Op. 119, No. 1 (adapted)

27.18 Hugo Wolf, *"Ein stündlein wohl vor Tag"* ("Just Before the Dawn") (adapted)

27. 19 Fanny Mendelssohn Hensel, *"Lust'ge Vögel"* ("Happy Birds")

27.20 Ludwig van Beethoven, String Quartet in G Major, Op. 18,
No. 2, mvt. 3 (Trio)

27.21 Joseph Haydn, String Quartet in F Major, Op. 74, No. 2, mvt. 1 (adapted)

Study the accidentals to determine the tonicized keys.

27.22 Wolfgang Amadeus Mozart, Piano Sonata in F Major, K. 332, mvt. 1 (adapted)

Rhythms Characteristic of Traditional Dances

Every culture's music is influenced by rhythms characteristic of its traditional dances.

Rhythms

If you don't know the feel of a dance, listen to one online and mimic its characteristics during your performance.

27.33

27.34

Melodies

27.35 Joseph Lanner, *"Marienwalzer"* ("Maria Waltz"), Op. 143, No. 1

27.36 Hans Christian Lumbye, *Britta Polka* (adapted)

27.37 Frédéric Chopin, Mazurka, Op. 33, No. 1 (adapted)

27.38 Traditional (Mexico), *"Pregúntale a las estrellas"*
("Ask the Stars")

27.39 Arcangelo Corelli, Sarabande

27.40 Frédéric Chopin, Mazurka, Op. 40, No. 1 (adapted)

Keyboard and Improvisation 27.3: Improvising a Waltz Using Chromatic Predominants N^6 and $A6$

1. Analyze the harmonies and write chord symbols below the bass pitches.

2. Have a partner play the accompaniment while you improvise a melody using the soprano as guide tones.

3. Switch roles and perform again.

4. *Quick Composition:* Notate your favorite improvisation. Create a score with a single staff for the soloist above a grand staff for the keyboard. Align the parts vertically. Switch with two new peers, who practice and perform your work.

CHAPTER 28

Chromatic Modulation and Ragtime

In this chapter you'll learn to:

- Perform music that features enharmonic modulations to distantly related keys
- Perform and improvise ragtime rhythms and melodies

Chromatic Modulation

Common tones, modal mixture, and enharmonic spelling are three ways to create a chromatic modulation.

Keyboard and Improvisation 28.1: Performing Chromatic Modulations

Perform each modulation type while singing the soprano part. Perform it again, augmenting the time values and using the soprano notes as guide tones for an improvisation.

For this modulation . . .	Perform . . .	How it works
Common-tone	mm. 1–4	$\hat{1}$ (I) becomes $\hat{3}$ ($\flat$VI)
Modal mixture	m. 1, then 3	Borrowed deceptive resolution becomes I ($\flat$VI)
Enharmonic spelling	mm. 1–6	m. 4: F respelled creates Gr^{+6} enharmonically

Melodies

In the first four melodies, play stems-down pitches while singing the melody, or sing as a duet with a partner.

28.1 V7/IV is respelled to become Gr+6

28.2 V7/iv is respelled to become Gr+6

28.3 vii°$^4_3$ in measure 4 is respelled to become vii°$^6_5$/V in ♭VI (G major).

28.4 vii°$^4_3$ in measure 4 is respelled to become vii°$^6_5$/V in vi (G minor).

28.5 Ludwig van Beethoven, Symphony No. 5, Op. 67,
mvt. 2 (adapted)

In this melody, the chromatic note E♭ is respelled as D♯, which is
the leading tone of the dominant in the new key, A major.

Andante con moto

28.6 Robert Schumann, *"Widmung"* ("Dedication") (adapted)

Innig, Lebhaft

Grab,   in das hin - ab ich e - wig

mei-nen Kum - mer gab!   Du   bist die

Ruh',   du   bist____ der Frie - den.

Translation: [O you, my] grave, into which I eternally pour my sorrow!
You are rest, you are peace.

28.7 Franz Schubert, 36 *Originaltänze*, D. 365, No. 3

Allegro

28.8 Franz Schubert, *"Wehmuth"* ("Melancholy"), Op. 22, No. 2 (adapted)

28.9 Johann Strauss Jr., Overture to *Die Fledermaus* (adapted)

28.10 Franz Schubert, *"Der Flug der Zeit"* ("The Flight of Time"), D. 515 (adapted)

28.11 Johannes Brahms, *Neue Liebeslieder*, Op. 65, No. 6 (adapted)

28.12 Ludwig van Beethoven, Symphony No. 4 in B♭ Major, mvt. 3 (adapted)

F is the common tone between F major (m. 21) and D♭ major (m. 22).

28.13 Franz Schubert, *Zwölf Ländler*, D. 790, No. 1 (adapted)

G is the common tone between C major and E♭ major.

28.14 Franz Schubert, Agnus Dei, from *Mass in A♭*, D. 678

A - gnus De - i, a - gnus De - i, qui tol - lis pec-

- ca - ta, pec - ca - ta mun - di,

Ensemble

28.15 Joseph Haydn, String Quartet, Op. 76, No. 6, mvt. 2 (adapted)

How would the chord in measure 14 be spelled in A minor?

Ragtime

Ragtime originated in African-American communities during the late 1800s. Characterized by its syncopated rhythms and slow march style, ragtime culminated in the music of Scott Joplin. According to Scott Joplin, rags should never be played fast.

Rhythms

Perform these rhythms in tempo giusto (strict time), without swing or rubato.

28.16 Scott Joplin, "The Easy Winners"

28.17

28.18

28.19 Scott Joplin, "Solace" (adapted)

28.20 Scott Joplin, "Bethena" (adapted)

Cantabile

28.21 Joseph Lamb, "Bohemia" (adapted)

Moderately

28.22

Andante

28.23

Moderato

28.24

Slow march tempo

Duets

28.25

Slowly

28.26

Waltz tempo

28.27 Scott Joplin, "Solace" (adapted)

Very slow march time

Improvisation 28.2: Improvising a Ragtime Melody and Accompaniment

1. *Solo:* Perform the accompaniment while singing the topmost notes in a comfortable register. Perform again, using the top line as guide tones to improvise a ragtime melody. Alternatively, sing your improvisation while listening to the recording.

2. *Duet:* Perform the accompaniment while a peer improvises the melody. Switch roles and perform again.

3. Choose one of these rhythmic motives and sing it often during the improvisation.

4. *Quick Composition:* Notate your favorite improvisation. Place the melody above the accompaniment and align all parts vertically. Exchange with a peer and perform each other's music.

Ensembles

28.28 May Aufderheide, "Blue Ribbon Rag" (adapted)

28.29 Daisy Allen, "A Bit O' Sunshine" (adapted)

28.30 Mynnie Dillingham, "Echoes from Old Kentucky" (adapted)

28.31 Marie Wilson Anderson, "Our March" (adapted)

Vocal Forms and Asymmetric Meters

CHAPTER 29

In this chapter you'll learn to:

- Sing melodies from operas, strophic songs, and hymnals
- Improvise a recitative with figured-bass accompaniment
- Perform rhythms in asymmetric meters with two unequal beats per measure

Opera and Oratorio

Operas and oratorios use a variety of vocal forms, including accompanied and unaccompanied recitatives, arias and cavatinas, and ensemble works for soloists and/or chorus.

Melodies

29.1 Wolfgang Amadeus Mozart, "*Voi che sapete*" ("You Who Know What Love Is"), from *The Marriage of Figaro*, K. 492 (adapted)

29.2 Gaetano Donizetti, "*Una furtiva lagrima*" ("One Furtive Tear"), from *The Elixir of Love*, A 36 (adapted)

Keyboard and Improvisation 29.1: Improvising an Accompanied Recitative

- Realize the figured bass while a peer improvises a melody set to the poetry of Alice Moore Dunbar-Nelson.

- To begin, play the given realization and use the suggested rhythmic outline for the text. Once comfortable, create your own, unique recitative.

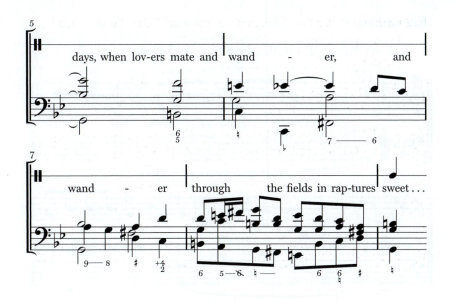

Ensembles

29.3 Henry Purcell, Recitative from *Dido and Aeneas*

29.4 Wolfgang Amadeus Mozart, *"L'ho perduta"* ("I Have Lost It"), from *The Marriage of Figaro* (adapted)

Translation: I have lost it, poor me! Ah, who knows where it is? I can't find it. I have lost it.

29.5 Scott Joplin, "The Corn-Huskers," from *Treemonisha* (adapted)
Treemonisha greets the characters who have come to husk the corn.

29.6 Dame Ethel Smyth, "Last Evening," from *The Wreckers*

Strophic Song

Strophic songs set more than one strophe (or verse) of text to the same music. Hymns and carols, folk songs, and popular songs are often strophic.

Melodies

29.7 Traditional (England), "With My Flocks"

Andante
mp

With my flocks as once I wan - der'd
Oft at - tain that way I wan - der'd

Gai - ly the moun - tains o - ver, Dam - sel
Hop - ing once more to meet her; Fan - cy

fair I saw ap - proach - ing, And with in - tent to
from the love - ly vi - sion, Oh! what on earth is

move her, I stept in her way, she passed me
sweet - er! But then, my poor heart is sad with

by, But ev - er my heart will love her.
fear, That I nev - er more may greet her.

29.8 Franz Schubert, *"Heidenröslein"* ("Wild Rose")

Translation:

A boy saw a wild rose
growing in the heather;
it was so young, and as lovely as the morning.
He ran swiftly to look more closely,
looked on it with great joy.
Wild rose, wild rose, wild rose red,
wild rose in the heather.

Said the boy: "I shall pluck you,
wild rose in the heather!"
Said the rose: "I shall prick you
so that you will always remember me.
And I will not suffer it."
Wild rose, wild rose, wild rose red,
wild rose in the heather.

29.9 Stephen Jenks, "Liberty" (adapted)

"Shape note" systems assign shapes (triangles, squares, circles, and diamonds) to different pitches to facilitate communal singing. Modern performers can sing the pitches and rhythm as with any other melody.

Asymmetric Duple Meters

Asymmetric meters contain unequal beats. A "5" appears in asymmetric duple meter signatures and the beats group either 2 + 3 or 3 + 2. To determine which, consider items like beams and articulations.

Rhythms

Tap eighth notes with one hand while conducting in two throughout. Make sure the beat durations change in measures of asymmetric meter.

29.10a

29.10b

29.11

Animé

29.12

Munter

29.13

Lent

Ensembles

29.20

29.21

Melodies

29.22 Traditional (England), "Barbara Ellen"

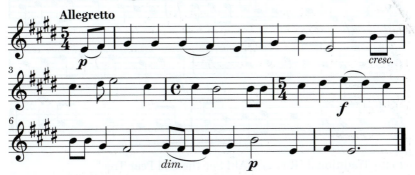

29.23 Traditional (England), "The False Young Man"

29.24 Traditional (England), "The Cruel Mother"

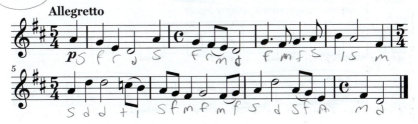

29.25 Traditional (Austria), *"Prinz Eugen"* ("Prince Eugene")

29.26 Traditional (Russia), "Ah! See the Old Pear Tree"

29.27 Béla Bartók, "In Folk Song Style," from *Mikrokosmos*, No. 100

29.28 Pyotr Ilyich Tchaikovsky, Symphony No. 6, Op. 74, mvt. 2 (adapted)

Sonata Form, Asymmetric Triple Meters, and Common-Tone Embellishing Chords

CHAPTER 30

In this chapter you'll learn to:

- Perform melodies from sonata-form movements and concertos
- Perform asymmetric triple-meter rhythms
- Perform common-tone embellishing chords

Sonata Form

Sonata form features a three-part design and a two-part harmonic structure. The form appears in many works: from symphonies and concertos, to vocal compositions, to solo instrumental sonatas, trios, and quartets.

	Exposition	*Development*	*Recapitulation*
Major key:	‖ I ⟶ V ‖	⟶ V	I ——— I ‖
Minor key:	‖ i ⟶ III ‖	⟶ V	i ——— i ‖

In the exposition and recapitulation, music from the primary theme (P), secondary theme (S), and closing theme (C) is often tonally stable, frequently featuring PAC cadences and periodic structure. Material appearing in the transition, development, and retransition is tonally unstable, featuring sequences, modulations, and motivic development.

Melodies

30.1 Aaron Copland, Piano Concerto, mvt. 2

Allegro assai

30.2 Gabriel Fauré, *Elégie*, Op. 24, for Cello and Orchestra

Molto adagio

30.3 Wolfgang Amadeus Mozart, Piano Sonata in G Major, K. 283, mvt. 2 (adapted)

30.4 Elisabetta de Gambarini, Sonata, Op. 1, No. 4, mvt. 1 (adapted)

Tempo di Gavotta

30.5 Wolfgang Amadeus Mozart, Piano Sonata in D Major, K. 284, mvt. 3 (adapted)

Andante

30.6 Sergei Rachmaninoff, Piano Concerto No. 3 in D Minor, mvt. 1

Allegro ma non tanto

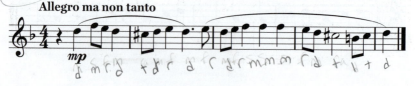

30.7 Johannes Brahms, Concerto for Violin and Cello in A Minor, Op. 102, mvt. 1 (adapted)

Allegro

30.8 Frédéric Chopin, Cello Sonata in G Minor, Op. 65, mvt. 1

Allegro moderato

Ensembles

When singing an instrumental part, switch to a comfortable octave to keep the instrumental line in your vocal range.

30.9 Joseph Haydn (?), Piano Sonata No. 15 in C Major, mvt. 1

Allegro

30.10 Joseph Haydn, Piano Sonata No. 14 in D Major, mvt. 2

Moderato

30.11 Ludwig van Beethoven, Piano Sonata in D Minor, Op. 31, No. 2 (*Tempest*), mvt. 1 (adapted)

30.12 Joseph Haydn, Piano Sonata No. 45 in E♭ Major, Hob. XVI:45, mvt. 1 (adapted)

30.13 Robert Schumann, String Quartet in A Minor, Op. 41, No. 1, mvt. 5 (adapted)

Part III Chromatic Harmony and Form

30.14 Wolfgang Amadeus Mozart, Piano Sonata in A Minor, K. 310, mvt. 1 (adapted)

Allegro maestoso

30.15 Wolfgang Amadeus Mozart, Piano Concerto in C Major, K. 467, mvt. 1 (adapted)

Allegro maestoso

Asymmetric Triple Meters

Asymmetric meters contain beats of unequal lengths. A "7" appears in asymmetric triple-meter signatures, and the beats group 3 + 2 + 2, 2 + 2 + 3, or 2 + 3 + 2. To determine which, consider items like beams and articulations.

Composers also express a meter of seven using changing meters, e.g., $\frac{3}{4}\frac{2}{4}\frac{2}{4}$, or by using dotted bar lines within a bar of seven beats.

Rhythms

30.16

Nicht schnell

30.17   2+2+3

Animé

30.18

Allegro

30.19

Modéré

30.20

Fast

30.26

Melodies

30.27

30.28

30.29 Traditional (Finland), "Home My Sweetheart Comes from Roving"

30.30 Joel Philips, "Holiday Round" (round in 3 parts)

Cel - si-us num - bers   make   ya feel numb - er

Fahr - en-heit win - ters   blow   it a - way.   Oh,

big - ger dig - its   don't make us   ee - jits.

Glo - ry   in   this ex - Cel - si - us day - o!

30.31 Robert Franz, *Wird er wohl noch meiner gedenken* ("Now, Will He Sometimes in Thinking"), Op. 23, No. 1 (adapted)

30.32 Gustav Holst, "Song of the Frogs," Op. 24, No. 6 (adapted)

30.33 Johannes Brahms, Piano Trio No. 3, Op. 101, mvt. 3 (adapted)

30.34 Maurice Ravel, Piano Trio, mvt. 4 (adapted)

Common-Tone Embellishing Chords

Common-tone embellishing chords (CT) prolong a major chord by embellishing its third and fifth with chromatic neighbor tones.

Keyboard and Improvisation 30.1: Performing Common-Tone Embellishing Chords

1. Play the progression while singing the soprano. Play again, this time using the soprano notes as guide tones for singing a melodic improvisation.

2. Now, play the progression while a peer sings. Switch roles and perform again.

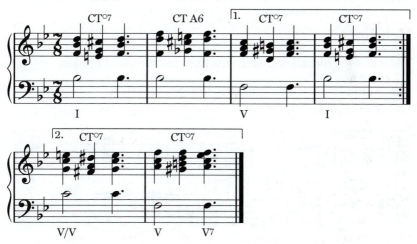

CHAPTER 31

Rondo and Three-Against-Four Rhythms (3:4)

In this chapter you'll learn to:

- Perform themes from rondo-form movements
- Perform three-against-four rhythms (3:4)

Rondo

One simple plan to compose a piece is *idea-contrast-return*: the **A B A** design of ternary form. Rondo form extends the concept, comprising three or more refrains separated by contrasting episodes. The more sections, the easier it becomes to create composite forms.

Melodies

The following melodies are refrains from instrumental rondos.

31.1 Anton Diabelli, Sonatina, Op. 168, No. 2, mvt. 3, Rondo (adapted)

31.2 Ludwig van Beethoven, Rondo for Piano, Op. 51, No. 1

31.3 Anton Diabelli, Sonatina, Op. 168, No. 4, mvt. 3,
Rondo (adapted)

31.4 Wolfgang Amadeus Mozart, Rondo, K. 485 (adapted)

31.5 Wolfgang Amadeus Mozart, Clarinet Concerto, K. 622, mvt. 3, Rondo (adapted)

Often, rondos are fast and lighthearted, but they may also be slower and contemplative.

31.6 Wolfgang Amadeus Mozart, Rondo, K. 511 (adapted)

31.7 Antonín Dvořák, Rondo for Cello and Piano, Op. 94 (adapted)

Allegretto grazioso

p semplice, mezzo voce

31.8 Johannes Brahms, Quartet for Piano and Strings, Op. 25, mvt. 4, *Rondo alla zingarese* (adapted)

31.9 Camille Saint-Saëns, *Introduction and Rondo Capriccioso for Violin and Orchestra*, Op. 28 (adapted)

Allegro ma non troppo

31.10–31.12 feature excerpts from Ludwig van Beethoven's Sonatina in F Major, Anh. 5 No. 2, Rondo (adapted). Melodies 31.10–31.12 present the distinct sections from Beethoven's **A B A C A** design.

31.10   Section **A** is the rondo's refrain.

31.11   Section **B**, episode 1, contrasts with the refrain. Following **B**, **A** returns.

31.12   Section **C**, episode 2, contrasts with both **A** and **B**. Following **C**, **A** returns.

Ensemble

31.13 Joseph Haydn, Piano Trio in G Major, Hob. XV:25, mvt. 3, Rondo (entire, adapted)

Three-Against-Four Rhythms (3:4)

To divide time two different ways simultaneously, multiply the desired divisions and choose a meter and beat division that allow both. Tap the following rhythms with both hands as indicated.

31.14

31.15

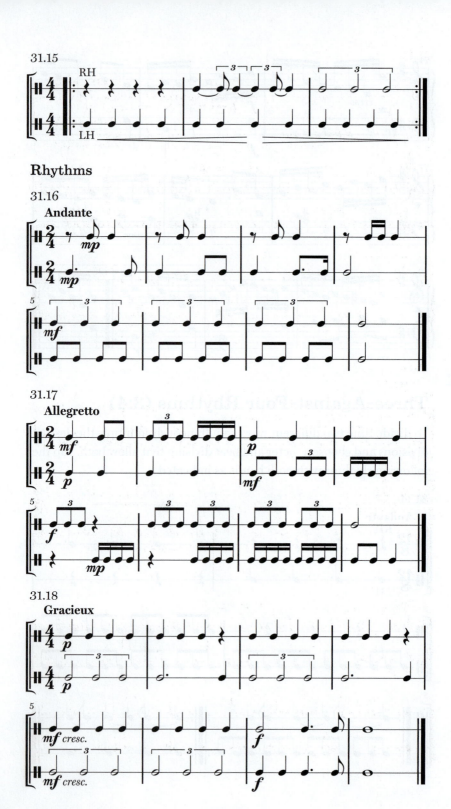

Rhythms

31.16

Andante

31.17

Allegretto

31.18

Gracieux

Part III Chromatic Harmony and Form

31.19

31.20

31.21

31.22

31.23

31.24

31.25

Keyboard and Improvisation 31.1: Improvising Using 3:4 Rhythms

1. Play this chromaticized sequence, which features four in the right hand and three in the left. As you play, sing the soprano. Repeat and sing the bass.

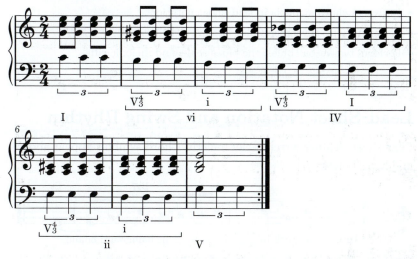

2. Choose a partner. One person plays while the other sings an improvisation that uses the soprano line as guide tones. Switch roles and perform again.

3. From 31.14–31.25, choose a rhythm and use it to perform the chromaticized sequence again.

4. Choose a different progression, like the descending-fifth sequence, and repeat the activity.

5. Perform as a trio to improvise a rondo that uses 3:4 rhythms. Person 1 performs the chromaticized sequence above as a refrain. Person 2 follows 1, playing a contrasting progression as one of the episodes. Person 1 performs the refrain. Person 3 performs a third progression as another episode. Everyone performs the refrain to conclude the rondo.

CHAPTER 32

Lead-Sheet Notation, Quaternary Song Form, and Blues

In this chapter you'll learn to:

- Interpret chord symbols in lead-sheet notation
- Perform swing rhythms in blues and **A A B A** songs
- Perform twelve-bar blues, the blues scale, and melodic riffs

Lead-Sheet Notation and Swing Rhythm

Lead sheets feature a treble-clef melody. Chord symbols appear above and lyrics below.

Tired of work-in'_____ soon I'll be home-ward bound.__

Lead-sheet chords indicate root and quality. A slash (/) means to play a chord over a specific bass pitch. The chart shows examples of how to realize lead-sheet chords.

When you see this chord symbol . . .	play a . . .
C or Cma or Cmaj or CM	C major triad
Cmaj7 or Cma7 or CM7	C major triad plus a M7 (B)
dm or Dmi or Dmin or d	D minor triad
Dm7 or Dmi7 or Dmin7	D minor triad plus a m7 (C)
Dm7/G	Dm7 chord over bass pitch G
Bø7	B half-diminished seventh chord
B°7	B fully diminished seventh chord
G7	G dominant seventh chord
G7 (♭9)	G7 plus a lowered ninth (A♭)
G7 (+11)	G7 plus a raised eleventh (C♯)

Swing rhythm is notated with simple beat divisions, but performed with long-short compound divisions, stressing the weakest divisions (shown with tenuto marks).

Written: Tired of work-in'_____ soon I'll be home-ward bound._

Performed: Tired_ of work-in'_____ soon I'll be home-ward bound._

Keyboard and Improvisation 32.1: Performing the Blues from a Lead Sheet

1. Keep a steady tempo and play the right-hand chords. With your left hand, play the root indicated by the lead-sheet chord symbol. Performers add notes to a lead sheet's basic chord symbols, as shown in this realization.

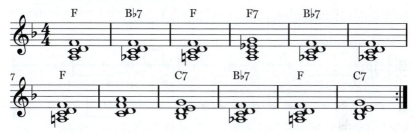

2. Choose an accompaniment rhythm and play it in every measure. Or, make up your own rhythm.

3. Play the progression while a peer improvises a riff during each four-measure segment. Here are two example riffs.

4. Play again while a peer sings a riff over the progression. Ask another peer to echo the riff to create a call and response. Take turns playing the progression and singing riffs.

Rhythms

32.1

Bright swing

32.2 Johnny Green, "Body and Soul" (adapted)

Slowly

32.3 Billy Strayhorn, "Take the 'A' Train" (adapted)

Medium swing

32.4

Medium swing

32.5 Antônio Carlos Jobim, "One Note Samba" (adapted)

32.6 Phil Woods, "Waltz for a Lovely Wife" (adapted)

Up

32.7

Easy swing

32.8 Thelonious Monk, "'Round Midnight" (adapted)

Ballad

32.9

Lazily

32.10

Fast swing

Duets

32.11

Fast swing

32.12

Up-tempo swing

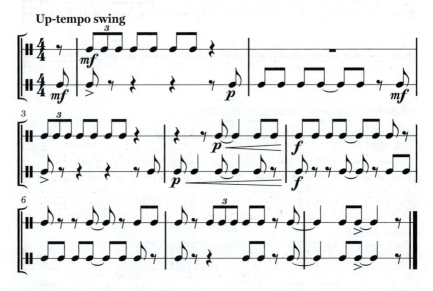

Melodies

32.13 W. C. Handy, "St. Louis Blues"

32.14 Clarence and Spencer Williams, "Royal Garden Blues"

32.15 Austin Lovie, "'Bama Bound Blues"

Sometimes swing rhythms appear as a dotted-eighth and sixteenth.

32.16 Thomas Wright "Fats" Waller, "Black and Blue"

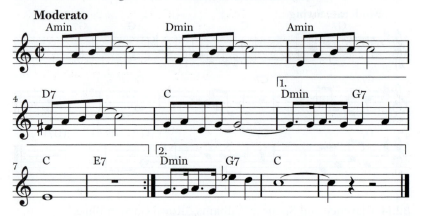

32.17 Hart A. Wand, "Dallas Blues"

32.18 Joel Phillips, "Rock Around the Corner"

Gon-na rock a-round the corn-er to night___ with you.___ The

boys and girls are gon-na come and rock a-round, too. The

mom - mas and the pa - pas gon - na

rock   a - long.___   Danc - ing and a - sing-ing this rock -
- in' lit - tle song.   Ba - by won't you join me?___
Ain't gon - na rock ya too long.___

32.19 W. C. Handy, "Memphis Blues"

32.20 J. Brandon Walsh, "The Broadway Blues" (adapted)

32.21 Joel Phillips, "Blues for Norton"

32.22 Austin Lovie and Alberta Hunter, "Downhearted Blues"

Trou - ble, trou-ble, I've had it all my days.

Trou - ble, trou - ble, I've had it all my

days. It seems that trou-ble's

going to fol-low me to my grave.____

32.23 Bradford Perry, "Crazy Blues"

Moderate Swing

32.24 Philip Braham, "Limehouse Blues"

32.25 Louis Armstrong, "Coal Cart Blues"

Quaternary (A A B A) Song Form

Quaternary songs usually consist of four eight-measure phrases with the design **A A B A**; **B** is a contrasting phrase.

Melodies

32.26 Jerome Kern, "Look for the Silver Lining"

32.27 George M. Cohan, "You're a Grand Old Flag"

32.28 George Gershwin, "Oh, Lady Be Good!"

32.29 Billy Myers and Elmer Schoebel, "You're Nobody's Sweetheart Now"

32.30 Bob Carlton, "Ja-Da"

32.31 George Gershwin, "The Man I Love" (adapted)

CHAPTER 33

Popular Song

In this chapter you'll learn to:

- Interpret extension symbols in lead-sheet notation
- Perform from rhythmic notation commonly found in popular song
- Sing popular song melodies

Chord Extensions in Lead-Sheet Notation

Popular-music chords often contain *extensions*, additional chord members equal in importance to the root, third, fifth, and seventh.

Extensions to major or minor triads

When you see this chord symbol ...	play a ...
Cmaj6, Cma6, CM6, Cadd6, C+6, CΔ6, C6	C major triad + M6
Cmin6, Cmi6, Cm6, C-6, cadd6	C minor triad + M6
Cmaj$^9_6$, Cma$^9_6$, CM$^9_6$, CΔ$^9_6$, C$^9_6$	C major triad + M6 + M9
Cmin$^9_6$, Cmi$^9_6$, Cm$^9_6$, C-$^9_6$, c$^9_6$	C minor triad + M6 + M9
Csus4, Csus	C, F, and G (the fourth displaces the third)

Extensions to seventh chords

When you see this chord symbol ...	play a ...
Cmaj9, Cma9, CM9, CΔ9	Cma7 + M9 (MM7 + M9)
Dmin9, Dmi9, Dm9, d9, d-9	Dmi7 + M9 (mm7 + M9)
Dmin11, Dmi11, Dm11, d11, d-11	Dmi7 + M9 + P11 (mm7 + M9 + P11)
G9	G7 + M9 (Mm7 + M9)

Extensions to dominant seventh (Mm7) chords

When you see this chord symbol . . .	play this chord . . .	plus the interval(s).	Optional interval(s)
G7(♭9)	complete G7 (G–B–D–F)	m9 (A♭)	
G7(♯9)	complete G7	A9 (A♯)	
G7(♭5)	incomplete G7 (G–B–F)	d5 (D♭)	M9 or m9 (A or A♭)
G7(♯5)	incomplete G7	A5 (D♯)	M9 (A)
G7(♯11)	complete G7	M9 + A11 (A + C♯)	M13 (E)
G13	complete or incomplete G7	M9 + M13 (A + E)	
G7(♭13)	incomplete G7	M9 + m13 (A + E♭)	

Keyboard 33.1: Playing Chord Extensions from Lead-Sheet Notation

1. A quick way to get satisfying voicings of extended dominant-function chords is to put the root, seventh, and third in the bass clef and the remaining tones in the treble clef. Spell enharmonic equivalents to indicate their direction of resolution (e.g., ♯5 goes up and ♭13 goes down).

2. Realize the following chords, voicing each several different ways. Some chords have four pitches, but many require more.

Bmi7   C♯maj9   F7(♭9)   A7(♯11)   A♭maj$^9_6$

Dma9   B♭mi6   E♭7(♭13)   Emi11   F♯13

Ami9   E7(♯9)   Cmi7   Gadd6   D7(♯5)

Popular Song

Rhythms

The following rhythms feature idioms and notational conventions common to popular song.

33.1 Euday L. Bowman, "Twelfth Street Rag"

Moderato tempo

33.2 Henry Creamer and Turner Layton, "Way Down Yonder
    in New Orleans"

Moderato

33.3 Charles Warfield and Clarence Williams, "Baby Won't You Please
    Come Home"

Relaxed

33.4 Fred Fisher, "Chicago, That Toddlin' Town"

Medium Swing

33.5 Irving Berlin, "That International Rag"

33.6 Lewis F. Muir and Maurice Abrahams, "Ragtime Cowboy Joe"

33.7 Jelly Roll Morton, "King Porter Stomp"

33.8 James V. Monaco, "You Made Me Love You"

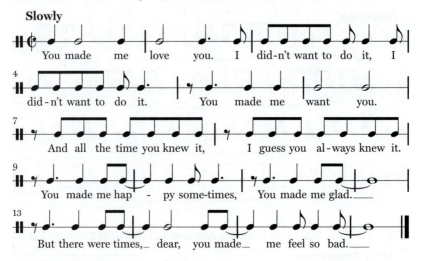

Melodies

33.9 Pete Seeger, "Turn, Turn, Turn! (To Everything There Is a Season)"

33.10 Traditional (Scotland), "Auld Lang Syne"

33.11 Joe Burke, "Tiptoe through the Tulips"

33.12 Don Hecht and Alan W. Block, "Walkin' after Midnight"

I'll go out walk-in'___ af - ter mid-night___ in___ the

moon-light___ just like we used to do. I'm al-ways

walk-in'___ af - ter mid-night search - in' for you.___

33.13 George Gershwin, "Fascinating Rhythm"

With agitation

33.14 Dave Logins, "Please Come to Boston"

Hey ram - blin' boy,___ now won't you set-tle down

Bos-ton ain't your kind of town___ There ain't no gold___ and there

ain't no - bod-y like me.___

33.15 Traditional (United States), "How Can I Keep from Singing"

33.16 Jerome Kern and Oscar Hammerstein II,
"All the Things You Are"

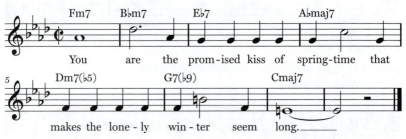

You are the prom-ised kiss of spring-time that makes the lone-ly win-ter seem long.___

33.17 George Gershwin and DuBose Heyward, "Summertime,"
from *Porgy and Bess*

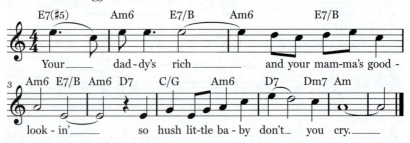

Your___ dad-dy's rich___ and your mam-ma's good-look-in'___ so hush lit-tle ba-by don't_ you cry.___

33.18 John Denver, "Annie's Song"

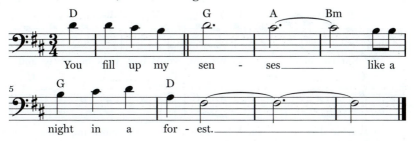

You fill up my sen - ses ___ like a
night in a for - est. ___

33.19 Traditional (Nicaragua), *Niño precioso* ("Precious Baby")

33.20 Sigmund Romberg, "Deep in My Heart"

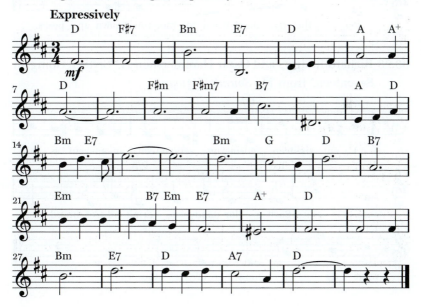

33.21 James Taylor, "Carolina on My Mind"

Kar-en she's_ a sil-ver sun,_ you'd best walk her_ way and watch it shine. Watch her watch_____ the morn-ing come._

33.22 Robert Henning and Heinz Provost, "Intermezzo"

Like the dream, you dream to-night, that fades from sight when dark-ness dis-ap-pears, may-be you will van-ish, too, the mo-ment when to-mor-row's dawn ap-pears.

33.23 Richard Rodgers and Oscar Hammerstein II, "Sixteen Going on Seventeen," from *The Sound of Music*

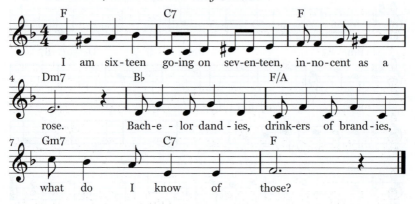

I am six-teen go-ing on sev-en-teen, in-no-cent as a rose. Bach-e-lor dand-ies, drink-ers of brand-ies, what do I know of those?

33.24 Joe Satriani, "Flying in a Blue Dream"

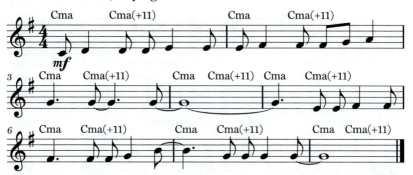

33.25 Paul Francis Webster and Dimitri Tiomkin, "The Green Leaves"

A time_____ to be reap - in',_____ a time_____ to be sow - in',_____ the green_____ leaves of sum - mer_____ are call - in' me home._____

33.26 Walter Donaldson, "My Blue Heaven" (adapted)

33.27 George M. Cohan, "Over There"

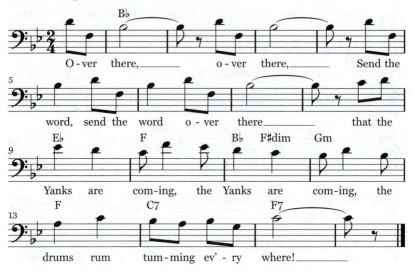

O - ver there,_____ o - ver there,_____ Send the word, send the word o - ver there_____ that the Yanks are com-ing, the Yanks are com-ing, the drums rum tum-ming ev'-ry where!_____

33.28 Irving Berlin, "When I Discovered You"

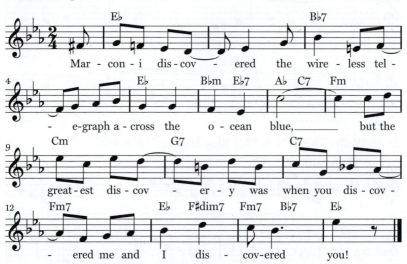

Mar - con - i dis - cov - ered the wire - less tel - e-graph a - cross the o - cean blue,_____ but the great - est dis - cov - er - y was when you dis - cov - ered me and I dis - cov-ered you!

33.29 Max Kasler and Gwen Wilke, "Free to Be Me"

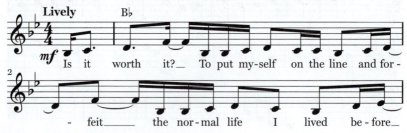

Is it worth it?__ To put my-self on the line and for - feit_____ the nor-mal life I lived be - fore__

this._ And I'm ner - vous._ It's te - ri - fy-

- ing,_ but at least I would-n't be ly-

- ing,_ 'cuz there's no use self de-ny - ing_ and I'd be

fly - ing free, Free to be_ me.

33.30 Jonathon Mount, "Bandaid"

Innocent ♩ = 96

It don't hurt e-nough for me_ to put a band-aid on.

I'm not sad e-nough to - night to be cry-ing on and on.

Fun - ny mov - ies won't cheer me up. There's

noth - ing that_ can be done for me, but

it don't hurt e-nough for me_ to put a band-aid on.

The Twentieth Century and Beyond

CHAPTER 34

Modes, Scales, and Beat Divisions of Five and Seven

In this chapter you'll learn to:

- Improvise phrases using major and minor pentatonic scales
- Perform historic and contemporary music based on or derived from modes
- Perform rhythms that include quintuplets and septuplets

Major and Minor Pentatonic Scales

The pentatonic scale consists of five pitches. In Western music, it is a subset of the diatonic collection and most commonly appears in major or minor form.

Improvisation 34.1: Improvising with Major and Minor Pentatonic Scales

Begin with the given measures and improvise eight-measure melodies that continue in the same scale, tempo, and meter.

Quick Composition: Notate your favorite improvisation. Include the correct key signature and meter signature. Exchange with a peer and sing each other's improvisations.

Melodies

Chapter 9 shows two methods for singing modal melodies. For relative solfège syllables, sing with syllables that apply to the major scale that has the same key signature. For parallel solfège syllables, call the centric pitch *do* (1̂) and sing with chromatic alterations.

34.1   Traditional (United Kingdom), "Edward"

34.2   Traditional (England), "Riddle Song"

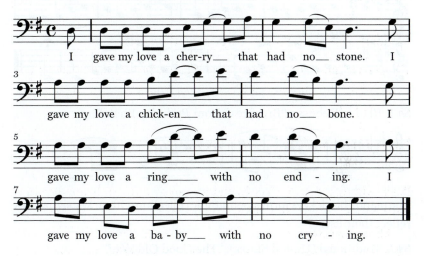

I gave my love a cher-ry___ that had no___ stone. I

gave my love a chick-en___ that had no___ bone. I

gave my love a ring_____ with no end - ing. I

gave my love a ba - by___ with no cry - ing.

34.3 Traditional (Thailand), *"Ngam Sang Duan"* ("Beautiful Moonlight")

34.4 Béla Bartók, "Evening in Transylvania" (adapted)

34.5 Claude Debussy, "Bruyères," from *Préludes*, Book II

The piano's black keys form a pentatonic collection. Often, key signatures reflect their use.

34.6 Traditional (United States), "The Good Old Way"

34.7 Joel Phillips, "Windsong," from *Pieces for Children*

34.8 Maurice Ravel, "*Laideronette, impératice des pagodes*" ("Little Plain Jane, Empress of the Pagodas"), from *Ma mère l'Oye* (adapted)

Diatonic Modes

After around 1900, composers developed new uses for modes. They transposed them, used them as pc collections, or intermixed them, creating, for example, the Lydian-Mixolydian mode.

Improvisation 34.2: Performing Modal Melodies

Begin with the given measures and improvise eight-measure melodies that continue in the same mode, tempo, and meter.

Lydian

Mixolydian

Quick Composition: Notate your favorite improvisation. Exchange with a peer and sing each other's improvisations.

Melodies

34.9 Traditional (France), *"Noël nouvelet"* ("Christmas Comes Anew")

34.10 Béla Bartók, *Fifteen Hungarian Peasant Songs*, No. 10

34.11 Yu Miyake, "Katamari on the Rocks," from *Katamari Damacy*

34.12 Traditional (Finland), "*Personent Hodie*" ("Let Resound Today")

34.13 Béla Bartók, *Fifteen Hungarian Peasant Songs*, No. 5

34.14 Ernest Chausson, "*La cigale*" ("The Swan"),
from *Four Songs* (adapted)

34.15 Koji Kondo, "Lost Woods," from *Legend of Zelda:
Ocarina of Time*

34.16 Germaine Tailleferre, Sonata in C♯ Minor
for Violin and Piano (adapted)

34.17 Philip Glass, "Evening Song," from *Satyagraha*, Act 3 (adapted)

Sing in four parts or play the dotted half notes while singing the melody.

34.18 Danny Elfman, theme from *The Simpsons*

34.19 Traditional, "*Ecce novum gaudium*" ("Behold the New Joy")

34.20 Fernando Largo, *"Cau'l Chouzano"*

34.21 John Lennon and Paul McCartney, "Norwegian Wood"

I   sat on a rug   bi-ding my time drink-ing her wine.

34.22 Béla Bártok, *First Term at the Piano*, No. 21,
"Farmer in the Dell" (adapted)

34.23 B. Mann, C. Weil, J. Leiber, and M. Stoller, "On Broadway"

34.24 Traditional (United Kingdom), "Famous Flower of Serving Men"

34.25 Rosemary Gurak, "Trending"

Ensembles

34.26 Béla Bartók, "In Dorian Mode," No. 28,
   from *Mikrokosmos* (adapted)

34.27 Béla Bartók, "In Lydian Mode," No. 37, from *Mikrokosmos*

The Lydian-Mixolydian mode consists of a whole-tone tetrachord plus a minor tetrachord.

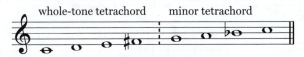

34.28 Joel Phillips, "Wallowtumble," from *Pieces for Children*
(adapted)

One person plays the bass line while two performers sing the upper
parts.

Beat Divisions of Five and Seven

Quintuplets and septuplets are indicated with or without a bracket and the numbers 5 or 7.

Rhythms

34.29

34.30

34.31

34.40

34.41

Duets

34.42

34.43

34.44

CHAPTER 35

Changing Meter, Symmetric Pitch Collections, and Slow-Tempo Asymmetric Meters

In this chapter you'll learn to:

- Perform melodies with changing and asymmetrical meters
- Perform melodies featuring symmetric pitch collections (whole-tone, chromatic, and octatonic)
- Perform slow-tempo quintuple and septuple meter rhythms

Changing Meter

Unless indicated otherwise, perform changes between symmetric and asymmetric meters using note-value equivalence (e.g., ♪ = ♪).

Rhythms

35.1

35.2

35.3

Andantino

35.4

Gracieux

Duet

35.5

Moderato

Melodies

35.6 Béla Bartók, *Fifteen Hungarian Peasant Songs*, No. 12

35.7 Maurice Ravel, *"Là-bas, vers l'église"* ("Near the Church")

35.8 Traditional (China), "Kangding Love Song"

35.9 Béla Bartók, *Romanian Christmas Carols*, No. 4

35.10 Ronald Hemmel, "The Piping Song"

35.11 Rebecca Clarke, Sonata for Viola and Piano, mvt. 1 (adapted)

This melody is in the mixolydian mode.

Chromatic Collections

Though some melodies comprise complete or near-complete chromatic collections, they often retain tonal associations.

Melodies

35.12 Sergei Prokofiev, Piano Sonata No. 4, mvt. 2 (adapted)

35.13 Hugo Wolf, *"Ein Stündlein wohl vor Tag"*
("Just before Daybreak")

35.14 Sergei Prokofiev, March, from *The Love for Three Oranges,*
Op. 33b

Tempo di Marcia

35.15 Nikolai Rimsky-Korsakov, "The Echo," Op. 45, No. 1 (adapted)

Moderato assai

Ensemble

35.16 Pyotr Ilyich Tchaikovsky, Symphony No. 4, mvt. 1 (adapted)

Whole-Tone (WT) Collections

Whole-tone scales comprise six pitch classes a whole step apart. The two WT scales, WT0 {0 2 4 6 8 t} and WT1 {1 3 5 7 9 e}, are literal complements.

Keyboard and Improvisation 35.1:
Performing Whole-Tone Scales

1. Play each scale up and down while singing with pitch-class integers.
   Avoid playing black keys with your thumb.

2. Identify the whole-tone scale. Then play it while singing pitch-
   class integers. For integers seven and eleven sing "sev" and "lev."

3. Choose WT0 or WT1. Choose a rhythm from 35.1, 35.2, or 35.3.
   Perform the rhythm while singing pitches from the collection.
   Create melodic interest by including skips and leaps.

Melodies

35.17

35.18 Claude Debussy, *"Colloque sentimental"* ("Sentimental Conversation"), from *Fêtes Galantes*, Book 2

35.19

35.20 Claude Debussy, *"La chevelure"* ("The Hair"), No. 2, from *Trois Chansons de Bilitis* (adapted)

35.21 Nonstandard key signatures can indicate the use of whole-tone scales.

35.22 Nikolai Rimsky-Korsakov, Sultan's theme from *Scheherazade*, Op. 35 (adapted)

35.23 Claude Debussy, "*Les ingénues*" ("Innocent Young Girls"),
from *Fête Galantes*, Book 2

35.24 Charles Ives, "September"

35.25

Duet

35.26 Béla Bartók, "Whole-Tone Scale," No. 136, from *Mikrokosmos*
(adapted)

Octatonic Collections

Octatonic scales alternate half and whole steps. There are three unique octatonic collections. Enharmonic spelling is common and one letter name must appear twice.

OCT 01 (includes pcs 0 and 1)

OCT 12 (includes pcs 1 and 2)

OCT 23 (includes pcs 2 and 3)

Melodies

35.27

Driving

mf

3

5

35.28 Alexander Scriabin, *Prelude*, Op. 74, No. 3

Allegro dramatico

f

3

5

f

35.29

35.30

Duets

35.31 Béla Bartók, "Song of the Harvest"

The dual key signatures correspond to the OCT 23 collection.

35.32 Béla Bartók, "From the Island of Bali," No. 109, from
   Mikrokosmos (adapted)

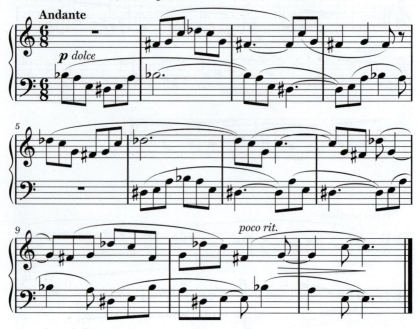

Asymmetric Meters in Slow Tempos

In faster tempos, quintuple meters divide into two beats per measure, and septuple meters into three beats per measure. In slow tempos, conduct these meters in five and seven.

Rhythms

Conduct slow-tempo quintuple meters using subdivided duple-meter patterns.

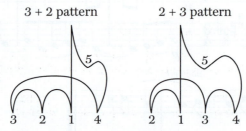

3 + 2 pattern   2 + 3 pattern

35.33

35.34

35.35

35.36

35.37

Conduct slow-tempo septuple meters using subdivided triple-meter patterns.

Duets

35.42

35.43

CHAPTER 36

Fixed-*Do* and Integer Solmization, and Spoken-Word Rhythms

In this chapter you'll learn to:

- Perform melodies using chromatic fixed-*do* solfège syllables or pc integers
- Improvise octatonic melodies
- Perform rhythmic settings of poetic texts

Chromatic Fixed-*Do* Solfège and PC Integers

These two methods for singing chromatic melodies have different advantages. Chromatic fixed-*do* solfège produces a purer vocal sound, while pc integers help when performing pcset analyses. With integers, sing *sev* for 7, *t* or *ten* for 10, and *e* or *lev* for 11.

Solfège:	*do*	*di*	*re*	*ri*	*mi*	*fa*	*fi*	*sol*	*si*	*la*	*li*	*ti*	*do*
pc integers:	0	1	2	3	4	5	6	7	8	9	t	e	0

Solfège:	*do*	*ti*	*te*	*la*	*le*	*sol*	*se*	*fa*	*mi*	*me*	*re*	*ra*	*do*
pc integers:	0	e	t	9	8	7	6	5	4	3	2	1	0

Keyboard 36.1: Playing Pitch Classes and Sets from Integer Notation

1. Play and sing the following pitch classes: 6 2 8 e 1

2. Play the following sets in ascending and descending order, and then simultaneously.

2 6	0 7	2 e	4 5	1 t
3 7 t	2 5 9	6 9 0	1 5 9	0 4 7
7 e 2 5	2 5 9 0	0 4 7 e	1 3 7 t	e 2 5 9

Melodies

Compare the use of solfège syllables, scale-degree numbers, and integers, and determine the most useful system for each.

36.1 Béla Bartók, *Mikrokosmos*, Book 5, No. 128

36.2 Maurice Ravel, *"Aousa!"* from *Chansons madécasses* (adapted)

36.3 Sergei Prokofiev, "Poem," Op. 23, No. 5

36.4 Max Reger, *"Der Tod, das ist die kühle Nacht"* ("Death Is the Cool Night") (adapted)

Der Tod, das ist die küh-le Nacht, das Le-ben ist der schwü-le Tag.

Translation: Death is the cool night; life is the sultry day.

36.5 Sergei Prokofiev, *Visions fugitives*, No. 13, Op. 22 (adapted)

36.6 Sergei Prokofiev, *"Legenda,"* from *Ten Pieces*, Op. 12 (adapted)

36.7 Sergei Prokofiev, Melody 1, from *Five Melodies*, Op. 35 (adapted)

36.8 Sergei Prokofiev, Melody 4, from *Five Melodies*, Op. 35 (adapted)

For these excerpts sing the mode, then the melody.

36.9 Béla Bartók, *44 Duets*, No. 10

Bartók uses a mode that is a rotation of A harmonic minor, centered on E.

36.10 Béla Bartók, *44 Duets*, No. 7

Bartók's mode rotates A harmonic minor to center on D.

36.11 Igor Stravinsky, *"Danse infernale de tous les sujets de Kachtcheï"* ("Dance of King Kachtcheï's Subjects"), from *L'Oiseau de feu* (The Firebird) (adapted)

Stravinsky's mode rotates E harmonic minor to center on B.

36.12 Anton Webern, *"Helle Nacht"* ("Bright Night"), from *Five Songs after Poems by Richard Dehmel*

36.13 Hugo Wolf, "*In der Frühe*" ("At the Dawn")

innig und zart

pp *allmählig verklingend*

36.14 Lili Boulanger, "*Nous nous aimerons tant*"
("We Will Love Each Other So Much")

tres ému et très contenu

Lent

à l'aise

sans nuances

36.15 Anton Webern, *Am Ufer* ("On the Shore"), from
Five Songs after Poems by Richard Dehmel

36.16 Alban Berg, *Liebesode* ("Ode of Love"),
from *Seven Early Songs*

36.17 Béla Bartók, *44 Duets*, No. 44 (adapted)

Duet

36.18 Béla Bartók, "Chromatics," No. 54 from *Mikrokosmos* (adapted)

Improvisation 36.2: Improvising Octatonic Melodies

Choose a rhythm. Choose an octatonic scale: OCT 01, 12, or 23. Improvise a melody by singing pitches from the scale with your chosen rhythm. Sing with integers or chromatic fixed-*do* solfège.

Sample improvisation using octatonic 01 and rhythm (3):

Quick Composition: Notate your favorite improvisation using accidentals or a nontraditional key signature. Exchange with a peer and sing each other's melodies with pc integers or chromatic fixed-*do* solfège syllables.

Rhythms of the Spoken Word

Poetic text may be set with a regular meter and rhythm, and in ways that either imitate or contradict regular speech patterns.

Rhythms

36.19 Madison Julius Cawein, "A Song of Cheer"

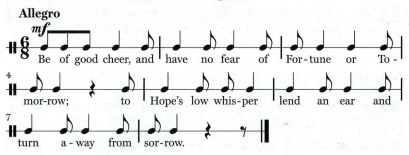

36.20 Ben Jonson, "An Elegy"

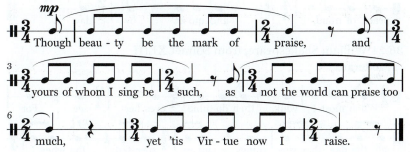

36.21 Ella Wheeler Wilcox, "A Dirge"

Calmly

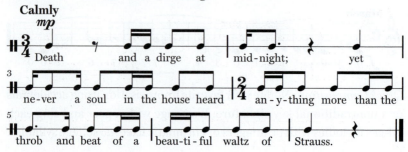

Death and a dirge at mid-night; yet

ne-ver a soul in the house heard an-y-thing more than the

throb and beat of a beau-ti-ful waltz of Strauss.

36.22 Robert Frost, from "Dust of Snow"

Moderately slow

The way a crow shook down on me The dust of

snow from a hem-lock tree has giv-en my heart a change of mood and

saved some part of a day I had rued.

36.23 Alexander Pope, from "Ode on Solitude"

(♩ = 120)

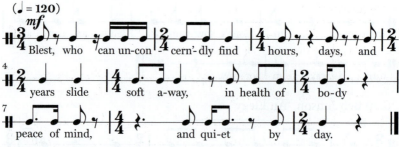

Blest, who can un-con- cern'-dly find hours, days, and

years slide soft a-way, in health of bo-dy

peace of mind, and qui-et by day.

36.24 William Shakespeare, from Sonnet XLIII

Moderato

When most I wink, then do mine eyes best see. For

all the day they view things un-re- spec-ted; But when I

sleep, in dreams they look on thee, And dark-ly

bright, are bright in dark di - rec-ted.

36.25 Christina Georgina Rosetti, "Song"

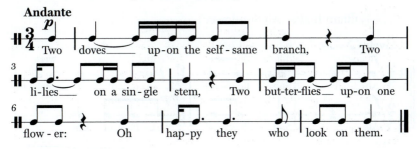

36.26 William Ernest Henley, from "Rondel"

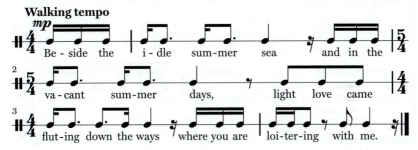

36.27 Thomas Moore, "A Canadian Boat Song"

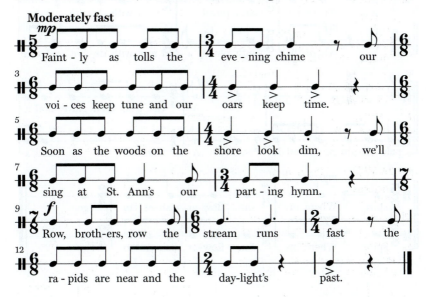

Duet

36.28 William Blake, "Ah Sunflower"

Trichords, Polymeter, and Obscured Meter

CHAPTER 37

In this chapter you'll learn to:

- Perform the twelve trichords in prime form and in inversions
- Improvise duets that alternate between whole-tone and pentatonic pitch-class sets
- Perform music with changing meters, obscured meter, or that is polymetric

---

Trichords and Prime Forms

A prime form is a normal-order set that begins with pc0 and represents all the transpositions and inversions of all sets in a set class. All trichord prime forms appear in exercise 37.1.

Keyboard 37.1: Performing Trichords and Finding Their Prime Form

1. Play the melody while singing with pc integers. Take special note of sets **A** and **B**.

2. Play the rotations of **A** and **B** to find the smallest span, or normal order, indicated with { }.

3. From the normal order, transpose the set to begin on 0. Use one of these methods:
   - Subtract the first integer from every element.
   - Call the first element 0 and count the semitones above it: 0 1 6.

4. Set **A**'s prime form [016] appears in exercise 37.1. But **B**'s pcs, 056, do not. When compared with its prime form, **B** must be inverted.

5. For inverted sets, play down from the top of normal order and count semitones from 0.

[0   1   6]

6. **B**'s prime form is [016]. Sets **A** and **B** belong to the same set class, which indicates that they are musically significant.

Melodies

37.1 The Twelve Trichords

Pitches 1-3 in each trichord are its prime form. Pitches 4-6 are an inverted form.

[026]

[027]

[036]

[037]

[048]

Refer to 37.1 (the twelve trichords) and follow Keyboard 37.1's procedure to identify trichords in the following melodies. Identify other important patterns too, like scales and modes.

37.2 Charles Ives, "Premonitions"

Slowly

p

37.3 Béla Bartók, "Dirge," Op. 9a, No. 2 (adapted)

Più andante

espressivo

mp

poco a poco cresc.

6

37.4 Sergei Prokofiev, "Poem" Op. 23, No. 2

Andantino

p semplice

3

dolce

37.5 Béla Bartók, *Two Romanian Dances*, Op. 8a, No. 1 (adapted)

37.6 Arnold Schoenberg, *Das Buch der hängenden Gärten*
(The Book of the Hanging Gardens), No. XIV

37.7 Alban Berg, Piano Sonata, Op. 1 (adapted)

37.8 Alban Berg, "Marie's Lullaby," from *Wozzeck*

37.9 Claude Debussy, *"C'est l'extase"* ("Ecstasy"), from *Ariettes oubliées* (*Forgotten Little Arias*)

37.10 Anton Webern, *"Himmelfahrt"* ("Heavenly Journey"), from *Five Songs after Poems by Richard Dehmel*

37.11 Anton Webern, *"Nächtliche Seheu"* ("Nocturnal Fear"), from *Five Songs after Poems by Richard Dehmel*

Duet

37.12 Béla Bartók, *44 Duets*, No. 28

Improvisation 37.2: Performing Whole-Tone and Pentatonic Scales as Sets

1. Place your left and right hands on a keyboard as indicated. Then play each scale while singing with pc integers.

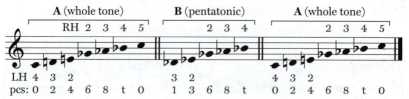

2. Use these sets to improvise a piece with an **A B A** design.
   - Choose a meter and a distinct motive for **A** and **B**.
   - Common tones 6, 8, and t create smooth connections between sections.
   - Create contrast: If **A** is loud, make **B** soft, if **A** is staccato, make **B** legato, and so on.

3. *Quick Composition:* Notate your favorite improvisation. Include a key signature or write with accidentals. Exchange with a peer and sing each other's music with pc integers or chromatic fixed-*do* solfège syllables.

Polymeter

Polymeter occurs when two different meters are played at the same time. Often, the meters move in and out of alignment with each other.

Duets

37.13

37.14

37.15

Obscured Meter

Obscured meter occurs when the perceived meter does not match the written meter.

Rhythms

37.16

37.17

37.18

37.19

37.20

CHAPTER 38

Pitch-Class Sets, Ordered Segments and Serialism, and Metric Modulation

In this chapter you'll learn to:

- Use pitch-class sets, ordered segments, and twelve-tone rows to improve performance of melodies
- Perform transformations of ordered segments
- Perform rhythms that feature tempo or metric modulations

Hearing Pitch-Class Sets When Performing Melodies

Recognizing familiar pitch and pc groupings can help ensure accurate intonation when singing a melody.

Melodies

Perform the pcsets, then use that sound to tune each melody as you sing it.

38.1 Arnold Schoenberg, *"Erwartung"* ("Expectation"), Op. 2, No. 1
This work opens with set [0 1 2 6] 4-5.

38.2 Joel Phillips, "*Haldī*"

This melody uses both all-interval tetrachords, [0 1 4 6] 4–Z15 and [0 1 3 7] 4–Z29.

38.3 Joel Phillips, "*Methī*"

This non-retrogradable melody is built on hexachord [0 1 4 5 8 9] 6-20.

38.4 Joel Phillips, "*Jīra*"

This melody employs Scriabin's "Mystic Chord" [0 1 3 5 7 9] 6-34.

38.5 Béla Bartók, Violin Concerto No. 2, mvt. 2 (adapted)

Listen for pentachords [0 1 3 5 7] 5-24 and [0 2 3 5 7] 5-23.

Ensembles

38.6 Maurice Ravel, *Le tombeau de Couperin* (Couperin's Tomb), Fugue (adapted)

Listen for tetrachord [0 2 4 7] 4-27 in the concluding stretto section of this fugue.

38.7 Joel Phillips, "A Crabby Canon"

38.8 Taylor Halpern, "Diverged"

38.9 Joel Phillips, "Adarak"

This melody uses the overtone or Lydian-Mixolydian scale, 7–34.

Ordered Segments and Serialism

Some themes are ordered successions with a distinct contour. One way to identify them uses ordered pitch intervals (opis), which record the direction (+ for up and - for down) and number of semitones between adjacent pitches.

Follow these strategies to transform ordered segments.

To create this transformation,	use opis that are ...	when compared with those of P.
P	identical	
I	the same, but have opposite signs	
RI	identical, but in reverse order	
RP	in reverse order *and* have opposite signs	

Keyboard 38.1: Transforming Ordered Segments

Play each given P_0, while singing it with integers. Then, use P_0's ordered pitch intervals (opis) to perform the specified transformation, like the examples below. If you find it helpful to notate these transformations, write on your own music paper.

Example

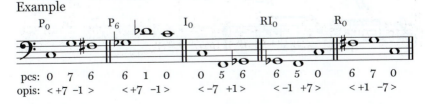

	P_0	P_6	I_0	RI_0	R_0
pcs:	0 7 6	6 1 0	0 5 6	6 5 0	6 7 0
opis:	< +7 –1 >	< +7 –1 >	< –7 +1 >	< –1 +7 >	< +1 –7 >

1. Given the opis of P_0, perform the specified transformation.

   (a) $< +2\ +3 >$ (b) $< +8\ -2 >$ (c) $< +3\ +4 >$

   $P_0\ P_3\ I_0\ R_0\ RI_0$ $P_0\ P_4\ I_4\ R_4\ RI_4$ $P_0\ P_{10}\ I_{10}\ R_{10}\ RI_{10}$

2. Given an ordered segment, find its opis. Then, find P_0 and perform the specified transformations.

   (a) $P_8\ P_0\ R_8\ I_4\ RI_0$ (b) $P_3\ P_0\ R_3\ I_2\ RI_2$ (c) $P_{10}\ P_0\ R_{10}\ I_{11}\ RI_{11}$

pcs: 8 _ _ _ _   3 _ _ _ _   t _ _ _ _ _

opis: $< \_ \_ \_ >$ $< \_ \_ \_ >$ $< \_ \_ \_ \_ >$

Melodies

Use the hints to determine the ordered collections
and their transformations.

38.10 Luigi Dallapiccola, *"Quattro liriche di Antonio Machado"*
    ("Four poems by Antonio Machado"), No. 1

This row's hexachords are subsets of octatonic scales.

38.11 Igor Stravinsky, Four Trios, from *Agon*

Perform the pitches forward and backward to discover how the composer organized his twelve-tone fugue subject.

38.12 Alban Berg, Violin Concerto, mvt. 1

The row, P_7, is the first twelve pcs. Measures 7–10 are I_7. Consider pcs 1–4 and 5–8 to be ordered segments: the second is T_2 of the first. Consider pcs 9–12 to be another ordered segment: the whole-tone tetrachord, 4–21 [0 2 4 6].

38.13 Arnold Schoenberg, *Variations for Orchestra*, Op. 31 (adapted)

Ensembles

38.14 Josef Matthias Hauer, Clarinet Quintet, Op. 26, mvt. 1 (adapted)

38.15 Arnold Schoenberg, *"Unentrinnbar"* ("Inescapable"), from *Four Easy Pieces for Mixed Chorus*, Op. 27, No. 1

38.16 Arnold Schoenberg, *Suite for Piano*, Op. 25, Trio

38.17 Arnold Schoenberg, *De profundis*, Op. 50B

Translation: Out of the depths I call to you, God.

Tempo and Metric Modulation

Tempo or metric modulation occurs when beat- and note-value equivalence are used to change the tempo or meter of a composition.

Rhythms

These rhythms use both simple- and compound-beat divisions to change tempo and meter.

38.18

38.19

38.20

38.21

38.22

38.23

38.24

38.25

The following rhythms use tuplets to change tempo and meter.

38.26

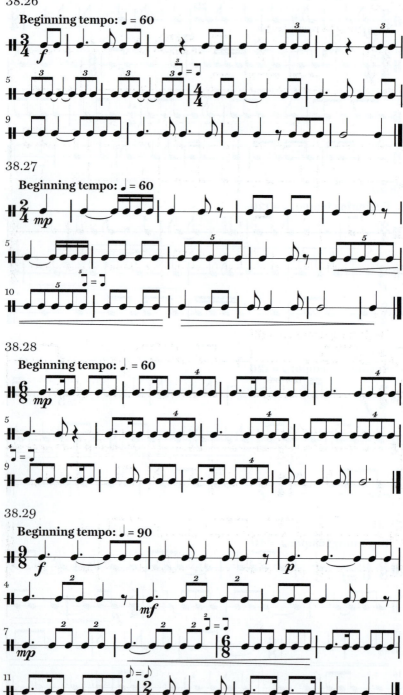

38.27

38.28

38.29

Ensembles

38.30

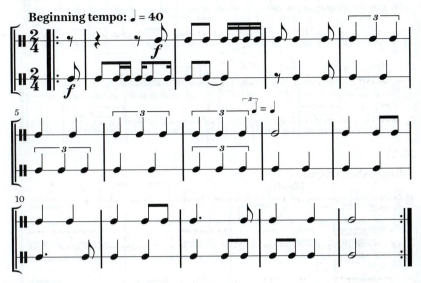

38.31

38.32

Beginning tempo: ♩ = 90

38.33

Assez vif

CHAPTER 39

Polymeter, Ametric Meter, and Non-Retrogradable Rhythms

In this chapter you'll learn to:

- Improvise a polymetric duet
- Perform ametric and non-retrogradable rhythms
- Perform melodies that include these rhythmic challenges

Polymeter, Ametric Meter, and Non-Retrogradable Rhythms

Polymeter occurs when two or more meters are present at the same time. Ametric music has no meter signature. Non-retrogradable rhythms sound the same whether performed forward or backward.

Improvisation 39.1: Performing Polymetric Ensembles

1. Each performer chooses a different pattern and prepares to perform it in a loop.

(a)   (b)   (c)   (d)

Using identical beat durations for ♩ and ♩., count off and begin performing together. Performers should conduct and emphasize the meter of their chosen pattern.

2. Perform again, but this time, one person begins and the other(s) enter(s) one beat later.

Rhythms

Tap the smallest note value and sing multiples of this value.

39.1

Vif

39.2

Calmly

39.3

Moderately

39.4

Fast

The next rhythms are non-retrogradable.

39.5

Assez vite

39.6

39.7

Slowly

A short note or rest is sometimes used to disrupt the regularity of the rhythm or meter. Such rhythms containing "added values" can appear in ametric music.

39.8

Calmly

39.9

Moderato

39.10

Moderately slow

39.11

39.12

Steadily

Duet

39.13

Vite (A)

Vite (B)

Melodies

39.14 Igor Stravinsky, "Royal March," from *L'histoire du soldat* (adapted)

Lydian mode

39.15 Béla Bartók, "Old Tune," No. 4, from
Fifteen Hungarian Peasant Songs

39.16 Béla Bartók, Ballad, No. 6, from *Fifteen*
*Hungarian Peasant Song*s (adapted)

39.17 Igor Stravinsky, Theme and Variations, from *Octet for Wind Instruments* (adapted)

Octatonic scale

39.18 Katharine Barry and Lilian Scott, "The Flower That You Gave Me"

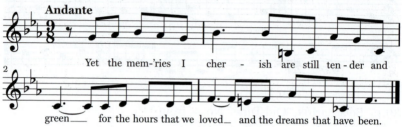

Yet the mem-'ries I cher - ish are still ten - der and green___ for the hours that we loved___ and the dreams that have been.

39.19 Oliver Messiaen, *"Danse de la fureur"* ("Dance of Fury"), from *Quatour pour le fin du temps*

Measures 1–4 are predominantly whole tone, and measures 5–6 are octatonic.

39.20 Anton Webern, *"Dies ist ein Lied für dich allein"* ("This Is a Song for You Alone"), from *Five Songs from "Der siebente Ring" of Stefan George*

39.21 Anton Webern, *"Im Morgentaun"* ("In the Morning Dew"), from *Five Songs from "Der siebente Ring" of Stefan George*

39.22 Paul Hindemith, *Concert Music for Strings and Brass*, Op. 50

Listen for subsets of the octatonic scale.

39.23 Alban Berg, *Lyric Suite*, mvt. 1 (adapted)

39.24 Anton Webern, *"In der Fremde"* ("In a Foreign Land"), from
    Four Songs for Soprano and Orchestra, Op. 13

39.25 Joel Phillips, *"La Flèche"*

39.26 Anton Webern, *"Ave Regina Coelorum"* ("Hail, Queen of
    Heaven"), Op. 18, No. 3

There are three row forms: P_4, I_4, and RI_4. The last pc of I_4
($G\sharp$, in m. 7) is also the first pc of RI_4.

Ensembles

39.27 Joel Phillips, "Holiday Round 2009" (round in three parts)

This melody is also Dorian.

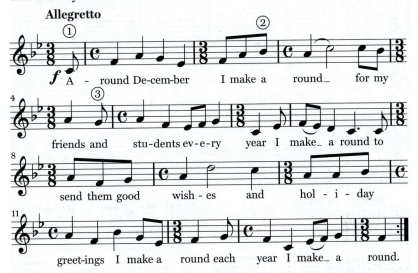

39.28 Erik Satie, *"Ogives"* ("Pointed Arches"), No. III (adapted)

39.29 Béla Bartók, *44 Duets*, No. 29

This melody moves from Dorian to Mixolydian.

39.30 Béla Bartók, *44 Duets*, No. 30

Allegro meno mosso

39.31 Béla Bartók, *44 Duets*, No. 19

Molto tranquillo

39.32 Joel Phillips, *Wild Nights!* (adapted)

This melody is based on the minor pentatonic scale.

Wild nights! Wild nights! Were I with   thee, *mp*

Wild___

39.33 Igor Stravinsky, Gloria, from *Mass*

Rhythm as a Structural Element and Non-Traditional Rhythmic Notation

CHAPTER 40

In this chapter you'll learn to:

- Perform isorhythms and improvise an isorhythmic dance
- Perform serialized rhythm durations
- Perform non-traditional rhythm notations
- Apply these principles to literature rhythms and melodies

Using Rhythm as a Structural Element

There are many ways to use rhythm as a structural element in music. Here are some of them.

Isorhythm:	Rhythmic pattern that repeats in the same part throughout a work
Serialization:	Associating rhythm duration with a recurring series, like a row
Golden mean:	Using the proportion .618:1 to mark significant durational events
Fibonacci numbers:	Infinite series that begins 1, 1, 2, 3, 5, 8, 13, . . . Each number is the sum of its two predecessors; adjacent numbers approximate the golden mean (e.g., 8/13 = .615)
Cipher:	Deriving values from an external source, e.g., the dots and dashes of Morse code
Groove:	The "feel" of popular music, often associated with characteristic rhythms

Duets

Exercises 40.1–40.3 feature isorhythms.

40.1 Isabel Giorno, "*Cuciando*"

40.2 Ivanna Odplavati, "*Mali Kos*"

40.3 Joel Phillips, "*Ben ritmico*"

Compare with Alban Berg, *Wozzeck*, Op. 7, Act III, Scene 3, "Invention on a Rhythm"

40.4 Anita Compari, *"Ándale!"*

Serialized durations, like serialized pitches, can appear in their original form and in retrograde.

40.5 Élleva Naidía, *"É Solo Mio"*

The ordered pitch intervals of [0 1 4 6] can be the basis for an isorhythm.

40.6 Joel Phillips, "Ciphernetic"

Here the rhythm values derive from Morse code.

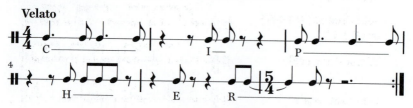

40.7 Joel Phillips, "Golden Meanie"

This rhythm uses both Fibonacci numbers and the golden mean.

40.8 "The Purdie Shuffle" (adapted from Bernard Purdie)

Steely Dan's "Babylon Sisters" and Led Zeppelin's "Fool in the Rain" feature a similar drum groove. Use your hands to perform the hi-hat and snare and your foot to perform the kick drum.

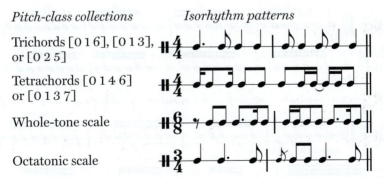

Improvisation 40.1: Performing an Isorhythmic Dance

1. From the choices provided, select a pc collection and an isorhythm pattern. On a pitched instrument, combine the pcset and isorhythm to improvise a dance. These are pcs; realize them as pitches using the full range of your instrument.

Pitch-class collections   *Isorhythm patterns*

Trichords [0 1 6], [0 1 3], or [0 2 5]

Tetrachords [0 1 4 6] or [0 1 3 7]

Whole-tone scale

Octatonic scale

2. *Quick Composition:* Notate your favorite improvisation using accidentals only. Add dynamic and other markings to convey the character. Exchange with a peer and perform each other's work.

Non-Traditional Rhythmic Notations

Some newer ways to capture the proportion of sound and silence include the following.

Feathered beaming:	Beam angle indicates rhythmic acceleration and deceleration, < and >, respectively
Stemless note heads:	Closed and open note heads indicate short and long values
Piano roll notation:	Horizonal bar length indicates duration (vertical placement is the pitch)
"Boxed" music:	A metered or unmetered figure boxed between repeat signs
Graphic notation:	Pictures are keyed to performance notes regarding their interpretation
Time-line notation:	Events occur as approximations along a time line marked in seconds

Rhythms

In exercises 40.9–40.12, conduct and keep a steady tempo. Where there are feathered beams, accelerate or decelerate within each quarter-note beat.

40.9

Moderately slow

40.10

40.11

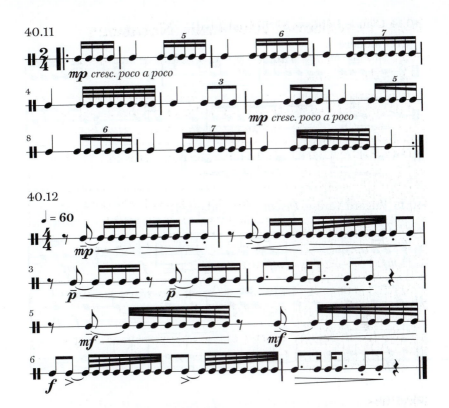

40.12

40.13

Focus on the rhythm of this composition, which combines many types of non-traditional notation. Where there are pitches, just approximate the contour.

40.14 Claude Debussy, *Syrinx* (adapted)

Très modéré

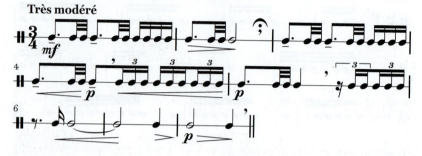

40.15 Edgard Varèse, *Density 21.5* (adapted)

40.16 Elliott Carter, *Eight Etudes and a Fantasy for Woodwind Quartet*, No. 9, Fantasy (adapted)

Tempo giusto (♩ = 84)

40.17 Luigi Dallapiccola, *Goethe-Lieder*, No. 2 (adapted)

Sostenuto: declamando (♩ = 58)

Ensembles

40.18

40.19 Charles Ives, Sonata for Violin and Piano, mvt. 3, "The Revival" (adapted)

Allegro con moto

Melodies

40.20 George Crumb, "Dark Mother Always Gliding Near with Soft Feet"

40.21 Sean Doyle, from *A Satire to Decay*

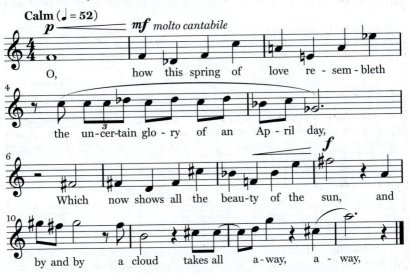

Calm (♩ = 52)

p ——— *mf molto cantabile*

O, how this spring of love re-sem-bleth

the un-cer-tain glo-ry of an Ap-ril day,

Which now shows all the beau-ty of the sun, and

by and by a cloud takes all a-way, a-way,

40.22 Morton Gould, *Jekyll and Hyde Variations for Orchestra*

If the excerpt were to continue, which pitch class would occur next?

p very sustained

held back

40.23 Deborah Koenigsberg, String Quartet, mvt. 3 (adapted)

40.24 Rebecca Oswald, *Finding the Murray River*

40.25 Andrew Ardizzoia, "Alone," text by Edgar Allan Poe

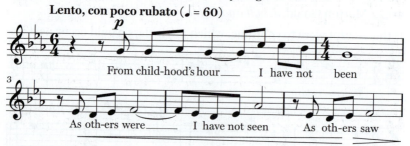

From child-hood's hour___ I have not been
As oth-ers were___ I have not seen As oth-ers saw

I could not bring my pas-ions from a com-mon spring. From the same source I have not ta - ken My sor - row; My sor-row I could not_ a-wa-ken my heart to joy at the same tone; And all I lov'd, And all I lov'd And all I lov'd___ I lov'd a - lone.

40.26 Sean Doyle, from *Samaritan* (adapted)

I am tired. I am tired of speech___ and ac - tion_____ I am tired.___ If you should meet me___ up-on the street do not ques-tion me for I can tell you on - ly my name_ and the name of the town I was born in___ ___ but that is e - nough.

Ensembles

40.27 Joel Phillips, "Reflections," from *Pieces for Children* (adapted)

40.28 Andrew Carter, *Nunc dimittis* (Now Let Your Servant Depart)

40.29 Howard Hanson, "How Excellent Thy Name"

40.30 Joel Phillips, "Two Lazy Cats," from *Pieces for Children*

40.31 Samuel Adler, *Psalm*

40.32 Joel Phillips, *Libera me, Domine!* (Deliver Me, Lord!)

40.33 Joel Phillips, "Gambolroister," from *Pieces for Children* (adapted)

This free use of all diatonic pitches is called pandiatonicism.

40.34 Leonard Bernstein, *Kaddish* (Symphony No. 3) (adapted)

This work features a twelve-tone ground bass set to an asymmetrical meter.

40.35 Luigi Dallapiccola, *Quaderno musicale di Annalibera* (Musical Notebook of Annalibera), No. 4

Treat this melody as a duet, or play one part while singing the other.

40.36 Joel Phillips, *The All Too Big Throne of Heaven*

Credits

"Royal March," from *L'histoire du soldat* (*The Soldier's Tale*). Libretto by Charles Ferdinand Ramuz. Music copyright © 1924, 1987, 1992 Chester Music Limited, worldwide rights except the United Kingdom, Ireland, Australia, Canada, South Africa, and all so-called reversionary rights territories where the copyright © 1996 is held jointly by Chester Music Limited and Schott Music GmbH & Co. KG. Libretto copyright © 1924, 1987, 1992 Chester Music Limited. All rights reserved. International copyright secured. Used with permission. Used by permission of Hal Leonard Corporation.

Thomas "Fats" Waller and Harry Brooks: "(What Did I Do to Be So) Black and Blue." Music by Thomas "Fats" Waller and Harry Brooks. Words by Andy Razaf. Copyright © 1929 (Renewed) EMI Mills Music, Inc. Chappell & Co., Inc. and Razaf Music Co. All rights reserved. Used by permission of Alfred Music and Hal Leonard Corporation.

Anton Webern: "Am Ufer" ("On the Shore"), from *Five Songs After Poems by Richard Dehmel*. Copyright © 1966 by Carl Fischer, Inc. All rights assigned to Carl Fischer, LLC. Used with permission. *Cantata*, Op. 29. Copyright © 1957 by Universal Edition A.G. Wien.
"Helle Nacht" ("Bright Night") from *Five Songs After Poems by Richard Dehmel*. Copyright © 1966 by Carl Fischer, Inc. All rights assigned to Carl Fischer, LLC. Used with permission.